GOING LONG

GOING LONG

The Art of Long-Form
Improvisation for
Stage and Screen

Jo McGinley

APPLAUSE
THEATRE & CINEMA BOOKS

ESSEX, CONNECTICUT

APPLAUSE
THEATRE & CINEMA BOOKS

An imprint of Globe Pequot, the trade division of
The Rowman & Littlefield Publishing Group, Inc.
4501 Forbes Blvd., Ste. 200
Lanham, MD 20706
www.rowman.com

Distributed by NATIONAL BOOK NETWORK

Library of Congress Cataloging-in-Publication Data
Names: McGinley, Jo, author.
Title: Going long : the art of long-form improvisation for stage and screen /
    Jo McGinley.
Description: Essex, Connecticut : Applause, 2025. | Includes index.
Identifiers: LCCN 2024021948 (print) | LCCN 2024021949 (ebook) |
    ISBN 9781493077939 (paperback) | ISBN 9781493077946 (epub)
Subjects: LCSH: Improvisation (Acting)
Classification: LCC PN2071.I5 M375 2025 (print) | LCC PN2071.I5 (ebook) |
    DDC 792.028–dc23/eng/20240606
LC record available at https://lccn.loc.gov/2024021948
LC ebook record available at https://lccn.loc.gov/2024021949

∞™ The paper used in this publication meets the minimum requirements of
American National Standard for Information Sciences—Permanence of Paper for
Printed Library Materials, ANSI/NISO Z39.48-1992.

In memory of my beloved student
Jason Murphy

and

in dedication to my husband and improv genius,
Stephen Kearin

Contents

Preface: How I Got Here

In the early '90s when I was starting out as a young actor in San Francisco, I found myself looking for tools to use when facing the unknown in auditions. After hearing about the classes offered by Bay Area Theatresports (BATS) Improv, I signed up for a beginning course. I didn't plan on staying for long, but I enjoyed laughing with everyone in the class, and as people shared their plans to continue, I stayed on.

At first everything was so new I had nothing to compare it to, but at some point, after I moved on to their intermediate classes, it activated something in my nervous system: I became more fearful and tightened up a lot more. When we had all been on our feet playing games together, I had felt free to make mistakes. As soon as we sat down and two people started improvising scenes, suddenly there seemed to be a right way and a wrong way, and getting laughs from the audience for your scene felt like the goal. My teachers never said this; they simply encouraged good acting and heartfelt scenes. However, if the audience was quiet, it didn't feel like a success.

My only exposure to improv up to that point had been the BBC's version of *Whose Line Is It Anyway?* Now I know that is only one brilliant piece of the improv pie, but in 1993 I thought it was everything.

One day I heard fellow students discussing the improv group True Fiction Magazine. This group included many BATS Main Company Members and the man who would later become my husband, Stephen Kearin. I joined my classmates at the show and sat in the audience, mesmerized. The stage lighting and music were moody with platforms and stairs the improvisers could use. The lights dimmed, the music came up, and True Fiction Magazine took the stage. They solicited a suggestion from the audience to inspire what would become two hours of fully improvised interlocking stories, and I was enthralled. The actor-improvisers were good, the characters big yet believable. The improvised lights and music supported everything on the stage. We in the audience laughed a lot, but I was also fully immersed in the theatrical experience. It was like watching a high-wire act. I was tense watching the show but not because I was nervous for them. They seemed fine. They seemed loose, in control, and playful. "This is the style of improv that I want to do, I said to myself." I didn't know how to get that good. It seemed a million miles away, but now I had a direction and a goal.

I started taking private classes focused on improvised scene work and moved toward longer and longer stories. I soon joined Scratch Theatre. Scratch was a group that improvised three styles of stories in one evening. Being thrown into the improv deep end, I forged bonds of friendship that continue to this day. The 1990s were a glorious time to be in San Francisco. I lived in the Marina District in a huge, light-filled studio with the distant sound of foghorns. I booked commercials continuously so I quit my regular job. I was performing and teaching improv all around town.

Work opportunities flowed in, and as 2000 loomed, my husband and I decided to move to Los Angeles. We settled into the delightful Los Feliz area of LA, where you can walk everywhere, including to Griffith Park. It was a great transitional neighborhood as I adjusted to the loss of my life in the Bay Area.

There is a Vedic worldview that identifies three aspects of the evolutionary process: creation, maintenance, and destruction. I was in the creation phase when I said yes to that first improv class at BATS. For years after, as I perfected my craft, booked acting work, and met my husband, I was in a maintenance phase. I didn't understand that I was heading into a destruction phase when we moved to Los Angeles. I had relocated with a lot of confidence. I had a large cushion of savings and over a dozen commercials running. I would regularly go to the mailbox and return with a stack of residual checks. This easy money had made the move to LA possible. I signed with a new agent and was sure I would book more work soon.

Upon arriving in LA, in the first week, I received a letter saying that my largest commercial campaign was ending. This financial shock, the new experience of being landlocked (the beach seemed a million miles from Los Feliz), and my dad suddenly dying of a brain tumor made my first year in LA rough. I wasn't doing improv; I was new in town and grieving. During this dark time, my friend Dan O'Connor had an idea. He was the artistic director for a well-known improv company in LA called Los Angeles Theatresports (LATS). He received a job offer in New York and needed someone to run LATS improv school. LATS was in the middle of their own destruction cycle. After years of thriving, things had suddenly shifted. They didn't have a home base, and before Dan left town, he gave me an email list of students and access to the checking account to book class space. This moment of "Sure, I'll do it" began a journey that culminates in the book you have in your hands. I created a school curriculum that appealed to my narrative improv interests. I rented space in Los Feliz, allowing me to walk to work. This small container was to hold the narrative joy and creation that would spill out and connect a global improv community.

I started an ongoing, long-form narrative class on Thursday nights that became a creative laboratory for the exercises and genres contained in this book. This maddening, inspiring, narrative long-form would keep the improv candle burning until, in 2006, a small group of us banded together and transformed LATS into Impro Theatre, the home of narrative improv in Los Angeles.

This moment of change may be precisely where you are now. You love improv and have found improvising scenes challenging and creatively satisfying. I hope you can see good improv wherever you live, but you may want to shift from short-form improv and bring narrative improv to your community.

The narrative direction I am taking you in this book differs from True Fiction Magazine and The Harold. The Harold is a narrative form developed by the San Francisco group The Committee. It is a long-form improv format emphasizing patterns, themes, and group discoveries instead of a traditional plot or story. In contrast, I will introduce you to a three-act structure for an improvised play, film, and even TV show. You will learn several genres and what is required for different kinds of stories to build and captivate an audience. Improvising in specific genres will give you structure that will enable you to be creatively free within that form.

By the time I was several years into teaching my ongoing long-form narrative class, I had drawers of notebooks containing in-depth information on various time periods and exercises I had created for different genres. In addition, I had copious notes on shows detailing what had worked and what didn't. One thing you should know about me: I love organizing chaos. Give me your most disorganized mess, and watch me go. At some point, I had to gather all the ephemera under one roof so I put together an "Improvising Plays and Films" notebook for every ensemble member. That was the genesis of this book: a training manual for improvisers ready to shift from short-form improv to long-form narrative improv.

This book contains key information to dive into narrative improv successfully. It will guide you step by step as you shift from short-form scenes to longer narratives. It will illuminate what's been missing in your current ensemble. It will educate you on behaviors that make you less present and impact others. By the end, you will understand how to shape and shift your mind and body to connect to other performers, under pressure, cocreating a cohesive story. In part 1, you will marinate in the foundational concepts around the mindset needed to do this work. There are exercises for each concept for you and fellow improvisers to try on your feet. Part 2 goes deeper into important practices for maintaining presence under pressure and developing the connection you have with yourself and your ensemble. Part 3 includes templates you can use to create an improvised play, film, or television episode beginning with the rehearsal period and continuing onward to showtime.

This will require all of you: you will need to act, improvise, make up a story, and jump into the unknown with other improvisers to cocreate a one-of-a-kind narrative that will never be told in that way again. My goal for you at the end of this book is for you to teach yourself and others exactly how to build up improv chops to tell longer and longer stories together successfully. The nuts and bolts I give you will make perfect sense to your thinking brain. However, before I give you the tangible tools to cocreate a story on your feet, I will provide you with a foundational mindset to be your own eye of the storm: the palpable presence you'll depend on in the face of uncertainty by not trying to self-protect or control everything but staying in the moment, using reality as fuel for innovation.

This book gathers almost thirty years of notes and experiments that I know will guide you into this incredible art form. No matter where you live, you can shepherd your improv group or students into improvising a one-of-a-kind narrative. I wish I could be there with you, and this is my best attempt to introduce the building blocks as they make sense to me. This book is an invitation to look at improv through a theatrical lens.

Let's begin.

Acknowledgments

I am deeply grateful for every person and every improv experience that made this book possible.

Chris Chappell, my editor: You threw me a lifeline when I didn't know where to turn. I am eternally grateful. Your edits were insightful and spot on. This book wouldn't be happening without you. Thank you!

Patsy Rodenburg: Reading your book in 2005 and then working with you in 2012 gave me a foundation to experience and teach presence. The world is so lucky to have you and I am eternally grateful for you.

Kathryn Kay, founder of A Writer Within: I treasure our friendship and your insightful edits of this book that helped me get it in shape to pitch it to Chris. You kept me moving forward at your writing retreat in 2019 and all through the pandemic. So grateful for you.

BATS Improv, San Francisco: My first improv home and the introduction to a way of life and my husband. Key inspiration from Carol Hazenfield, Diane Rachel, and Rafe Chase.

ACKNOWLEDGMENTS

Scratch Theatre: Thank you for seeing potential in me and for the invitation to your narrative world. Kristina Robbins, Daphne Brogdon, Dave Dennison, Rob Rodgers, and Kurt Bodden.

Impro Theatre, Main Co., Los Angeles, 2006–2019: You gave me a creative laboratory and a life-long community. Thank you! Stephen Kearin, Dan O'Connor, Edi Patterson, Kelly Holden Bashar, Ryan Smith, Nick Massouh, Kari Coleman, Lisa Fredrickson, Brian Lohmann, Brian Jones, Lauren Lewis, Paul Rogan, Michele Spears, Floyd VanBusKirk, Madi Goff, Mike Rock, Mike McShane, Tracy Burns, and Paul Hungerford.

Nick Massouh: As the dean of Impro Theatre School you made the curriculum even better after I left. You also brought me out of retirement! I thought I was through teaching and you lured me back. Thank you from the bottom of my heart.

Impro Theatre, School of Narrative Improvisation: Thank you for the creative environment that brought out the best in all of us. What a time we had! *Passion Noir*, *Fosse Cabaret*, *Twilight Zone UnScripted*, *The Portal*, *Nancy Drew UnSolved*, *ABC Afterschool Special*, *Improvised Inge*, *Dorothy Parker*, too many to name—thank you, thank you. Jason Murphy, Carla Rosati, Kim Crowe, Glenn Camhi, Jim Babcock, Paul Hungerford, Matthew Pitner, Sara Mountjoy Pepka (Oceans 2 Forever!), Ahsan Butt, Paul Vonasek, Laurie Jones, Nick Clark, Kelly Lohman, Ted Cannon, Leanna Dindal, Eric Carthen, Rebecca Lowman. Jen Reiter, Kirsten Farrell, Alex Caan, Arlo Sanders, Emily Jacobsen, Cory Wyzynski, Jill Hoffman, Paul Marchegiani, Helen Hegarty, Andrew Pearce, Susan Deming, and Cory Rouse.

Carla Rosati and Jorge Narino: Thank you for the years of laughter and encouragement. I am so grateful for you and can't wait to be old-timers together.

ACKNOWLEDGMENTS

Kathy and Joe Rinaldi and Teresa Bueno: Without your steadfast encouragement and talent I might not have pushed through. Thank you, thank you.

Glen and Judi Eastman: Your belief in me and willingness to step in and offer support at key moments kept me going. I miss clam chowder Fridays and laughing with you both.

Misha Collins: You told me about Vipassana meditation and Patsy Rodenburg, therefore changing the course of my life. Thank you.

Mick Kubiak: A million laughs, insights, and unicorn magic. Sweet sister, I'm so grateful for you.

Kristina Robbins: My partner in travel and teaching. You consistently show me what a true friend is. Love you forever.

Improv Inspiration: Corey Rosen, Derek Yee, Karen Brelsford, Stephanie Dennison, and Hannah Levinson. Connecting in the pandemic and creating magic together at BATS kept me inspired and motivated. Forever grateful for each one of you.

Danny Slomoff: Your mentorship and knowledge has been life changing. Your wisdom changed my professional trajectory. Thank you, thank you.

Stuart and Jennifer Levinson: Laughing with you and your constant positive encouragement means the world to me. Can't wait for future adventures.

333 Communications: To all my coaching clients, you are the light that inspires me and gives me energy. I feel too lucky to have you in my life.

Michael Grazer and Stephen Lazar: Best neighbors ever. You made our house a home.

ACKNOWLEDGMENTS

To my mom Joan, and my siblings Sue, Brian, Keith, and Karyn, and in memory of my dad, Jack McGinley. Thank you for being there for me through thick and thin. To the Kearins and Blairs: Thank you for welcoming me into your families. I love each one of you.

Tamra Rutherford: You gave me a space to find the true connection and bravery that got me where I am today. You mean the world to me. A huge thanks from Big and Little Jo.

To my husband, Stephen Kearin. Meeting you set me on a life path full of laughter and adventure. I cannot imagine a better person to go moment to moment with. You are a light in this world and I am eternally grateful for you and the home we have created together.

PART I

THE GOING LONG MINDSET

1

THE MENTAL DISTANCE BETWEEN SHORT FORM AND GOING LONG

When I took my first improvisation class, I was very nervous. The room was raucous, and I didn't know anyone. Once we gathered in a circle and exchanged names, the room relaxed slightly, and I thought, "I can do this." It felt like we were on the same team and would support each other. However, as we felt the pressure to earn laughs for our improvisations, I felt that group connection splinter. Some improvisers started trying to push and control what we were doing, some pulled back and merely observed, and others floated somewhere in the middle. The cohesive feeling had broken apart. What had happened?

I believe our group connection splintered because beginning improvisers tend to get pushed into performing for each other too soon. We learn to listen, to say "Yes, and" instead of "No," and to make our partners look good, but often something else happens. We hear these foundational principles and heartily agree: "That sounds good. That makes sense." However, two minutes later, when on our feet in front of our peers, we will—seemingly against our will—say "No," not listen, or leave our partner hanging. We may understand these principles and want to do good work, but we do not have control over our reactions—*yet*. It's imperative to learn *how to be present under pressure* while simultaneously learning the fundamentals of improv. You need something tangible upon which to place the improv ethics. You need to engage in something more significant than the thinking brain.

"Presence" is a word that has been tossed around quite a bit over the past decade. It's a vague diagnostic term that can make you feel good or bad about yourself. "You have presence!" "You lack presence!" Well, how do I get it and keep it, many ask. Before discussing group connection and finding flow as an ensemble, which are the requirements of good narrative improv, we have to talk about the *individuals* who make up the whole.

If you are reading this book, I assume you already know how to improvise and want to shift from short-form improv to long-form narrative improv. Perhaps you have discovered that improvising scenes— good scenes—is incredibly satisfying. That feeling of connection with yourself and your partner cocreating a story can be exhilarating. I bet that there are scenes you've improvised that you still see in your mind's eye. You see the location, know how you felt, and remember a specific moment when it all came together. You may have noticed that there are certain improvisers you do better scenes with so you try to jump up onstage when they get up. You might think this narrative magic lies outside yourself and depends on various ingredients not within your control. As you shift from short-form improv and head down the longer narrative improv path, you have many skills that you are taking with you. Some will always come in handy (saying "Yes, and";

listening; and making your partner look good), but some may be detrimental to telling a longer story with fellow improvisers.

The Difference between Keeping It Short and Going Long

In short-form improv you are taught to jump in and rescue a failing scene. The scenes stand independently, and no connections to other scenes are needed. Characters can be big as we aren't spending too much time with them.

In narrative long-form improv, however, your goal is to create a three-act narrative in the moment with other improvisers that lasts 1–2 hours. The scenes that comprise the more extended narrative must connect and build upon each other. You want a riveting opening scene, a second act that deepens our interest in the story, and a satisfying ending on all levels. The main characters must be believable. We want to spend time with characters we care about because they create the narrative we are watching.

Is it possible for the skills of a short-form improviser to translate to long-form narrative improv? Absolutely. However, you must understand that you are applying your improv skills to a different form. It's still improv, but you need endurance. You need to sustain a connection with yourself, your fellow improvisers, and the story over 1–2 hours. You must expand your range and strengthen weak muscles to create a successful long-form narrative at the highest level possible.

In short-form, you can stand off to the side observing the scene and then enter with a big character, a funny line, and bam!—the lights go out. That makes it easy to end a scene that's not working. However, I know improvisers who lean too hard on this technique in long-form narratives. When I first improvised, we called this behavior "Hey, Kool-Aid." When I was growing up, there were Kool-Aid commercials where people would be in their homes, and suddenly a massive pitcher of Kool-Aid would burst through their wall with a smile on its face, and everyone would happily yell, "Hey, Kool-Aid!" I wish I could say I happily embraced the "Kool-Aid" entering our scene, but it often felt intrusive and judgmental when other improvisers did it, as if they were saying, "Your scene was boring, so I came in to liven it up or end it." This ability to enter a scene and say one line of dialogue that brings the lights down is a skill you can put on the back burner. Once in a great while, this may come in handy depending on the genre and narrative. Let it be one of your many tools, not the only tool you use.

In short-form, every scene or game stands on its own. In narrative improv, every scene builds upon the last. You must have a sense of the genre and who the current story is about while not forcing or controlling the way the story unfolds. You must be able to track narrative. Does this sound difficult? It is. It's imperative that everyone in the cast

1. Knows how to improvise.
2. Understands their response to anxiety and how to stay connected to themselves and others.
3. Develops a strong knowledge of the current genre they are improvising.
4. Takes the work seriously, but doesn't take themselves too seriously.

Assuming you've arrived with 1 in place, this book will help you with 2, 3, and 4.

Later in this book I'll discuss various genres and offer a template for an improvised play that you can use to learn story structure. Genres provide a backbone for long-form narrative. Without the guardrails of a genre, there are too many options or directions to follow. The lack of collective focus between all members of the ensemble can lead to disorienting decision fatigue. Genre gives the improviser a detailed toolbox to draw on, a shared point of reference so that all the performers have a sense of where they are going together. Studying genre also reduces the risk of a long-form story becoming too long, aimless, and self-indulgent.

Ultimately this narrative journey is supposed to be fun for you *and* the audience. This brings us to the difference between small laughs and full, sustained laughs. Certain off-the-cuff remarks in improv can be amusing and will make your audience chuckle. These are what I consider small laughs. It's interesting to note what these small laughs do to narrative energy. If you are working with improvisers constantly trying to get laughs throughout a scene, instead of increasing tension the laughs release it in a way that can diminish the power of the narrative. When actors are in a scene and the audience is engaged, there are times when the laugh is a relief, and we all let go. A skilled narrative improviser puts story and relationship first, though, and the laughs happen organically. Conversely, I don't want to be in the audience watching improvisers trying to be serious. I *do* want to watch a group of talented, connected improvisers cocreate a one- or two-hour narrative that is a riveting, one-of-a-kind experience. This is what has kept me coming back year after year.

With a long-form narrative, you must stay connected to the current story whether you are onstage or not. You need to hold what you *think* is happening very lightly in your hands and be ready to adapt as the narrative changes before your eyes. You might wonder, "How can I be in control and let go of control simultaneously? How can I immerse myself and respond without thinking while at the same time tracking the evolving narrative?"

Think of professional athletes. When watching the World Cup, you see a group of professional athletes playing at the highest level. They know how to play soccer but do not know how this game will end. They know they want to win, but they improvise at every moment of the game. They are watching the ball in play and responding accordingly. They cannot control every move. They are ideally in control when they have the ball, but other than that, they are watching and responding with a shared goal that connects them. Getting into that mental zone, and maintaining a connection with your ensemble, is the ideal that long-form improvisers need to aim for. I'll discuss how to get there in chapter 2.

Remember: When you're improvising a long-form narrative, what you are creating is in some sense the *final*, edited scene that the writer and director all agreed *must* be kept in a film or play. Nothing you say onstage is extra even if you don't know what you said; it's out there as part of the story and was therefore intentional. That's why every mistake can be welcomed and used to its full potential. The mistakes-are-gifts concept is pure magic and can transport all of you together.

While attempting to put a story on the stage, a powerful approach is to look at every constraint through the lens of "We can if . . ." Whether it's budget, stage dimensions, or merely being uncertain about how to make something look real onstage, tackle it with an open mind. "Can we make it look like the chairs are cars racing down the road?" *We can if* we isolate the chairs in a pool of light and the actors have rehearsed how to move together in slow motion. "Can we make the stage seem larger?" *We can if* the actors have trained to walk or run in place while looking out over the audience and verbally endowing the landscape, combined with lights and sound. You see what I mean. *We can if . . .* Get creative.

2

THE FOUNDATIONAL MINDSET
OF TANGIBLE CONNECTION

I had been teaching improv for about fifteen years before I learned of Patsy Rodenburg's three circles of energy. In 2005, I read her book *The Second Circle* and began applying it to my exploration of narrative improv. I wish I had known about second circle when I first started out. Back then I struggled to understand what presence was and how to replicate that feeling of being in the zone with another improviser. When I did well in a scene, I would try to figure out *why* it went well, but it was opaque. I tried to control whom I did scenes with because with those people I did excellent work while with "those other people," I did not.

Instead of trying to only work with specific performers, I should have been focusing on my own ability to connect with others and be at my best. As humans we all have physiological responses to fear, anxiety, pressure, disruption, and the unknown. These responses serve a purpose but may get in the way of improvising to the best of our ability. When faced with uncertainty, some of us tend to pull back: we want to get the lay of the land or suss out the situation before we engage. This is what Rodenburg calls the *first circle*, the circle of self and withdrawal.

Being in the first circle is somewhat like people-watching from a park bench. You are observant and paying attention but not engaging or expressing yourself. As an improviser, you might be on the side of the stage and overthinking about whether to enter the scene. You might be trying to figure out what will happen if you make this call or that call. In the meantime, while you are in your head, the scene has moved on, and you find yourself asking, "What did I just miss?" You may be trying too hard to get it right or afraid of failing—or, if you're in a class, you might want to avoid getting notes from the instructor. But this kind of self-protection will not make you a great improviser or fun to play with. As an improviser in first circle, you give nothing and can even take energy away from the ensemble. You are not sending signals of confidence to your fellow improvisers. If you are onstage in first circle, you may even be difficult to hear. Others will not feel your physical presence so you will have little impact on the room. You may feel you aren't doing any harm in first circle. After all, you are trying not to add to the confusion or make a mistake! However, your time in first circle will create an energy imbalance in the ensemble, and others may pull back with you or overcompensate.

In contrast, you may be the improviser who goes all-in instead of pulling back from a situation to self-protect or assess as in the first circle. This is what Rodenburg calls the *third circle* and it is the circle of bluff and force. You see a scene failing and jump in to try and save it. Or the scene is going fine but you have an idea for a character and jump right in with your potentially unnecessary contribution. Your fellow improvisers might be stuck in first circle, overthinking things and driving you crazy. Now you are taking things into your own hands and might not even be happy about it. You may think, "Once again, this is on my shoulders." The way you deal with your anxiety is to jump in and *do* something. Anything. Taking control and going down with the ship or saving the show is what you do.

There is a great strength to this willingness to take risks. However, when you are in third circle, you cannot easily sense the subtleties of your partner or the situation. Instead, you take hostages. You may make fellow improvisers feel you are talking *at* them rather than *with* them. You spray your energy around the room as if from an aerosol can. You may feel the success of the show or scene is on your shoulders, so you push on. Third is a difficult energy to sustain, and it can fizzle out because it's not grounded. The audience may start disengaging with the first or third circle performers because it requires too much energy to hear, understand, or connect with them. Watching performers onstage be ignored or plowed over by an improviser in third is also uncomfortable. I remember improv teachers trying to get shyer improvisers to break out of their shell by having them do huge and silly things. It would only work momentarily as the first circle improviser shot out of first into third, felt uncomfortable, and would snap back into first. Likewise, sometimes when teachers tried to get a third circle improviser to stop talking or listen better, the improviser would act like their superpowers were being taken away. It never stuck. They would listen better in that one scene and then go back to their comfort zone.

Both first and third circle are off balance. Imagine trying to ski down a mountain: if you lean too far back (first circle) or forward (third circle), you will fall. Whenever you learn a sport, you first learn the coordination system required for that sport. Your stance, balance, and breath alignment are usually taught first. You are taught the reset point that is your touchstone. You may never have questioned your knee-jerk response to uncertainty, but I'm telling you now, you have a choice. With awareness and breathing, you can choose your response to the unknown, the perpetual state of improv.

Suppose you are working with improvisers unaware of their habitual responses to uncertainty and how those responses affect others. In that case, you will be entangled in a push-pull relationship with half the improvisers onstage defaulting to first and the other half to third. This dynamic makes it very hard for you to truly collaborate, improvise together, or even enjoy the process.

So what *is* the state where we come together? It's what Rodenburg calls the *second circle*, the circle of connection. In second circle, you may feel as nervous as everyone else but you choose not to self-protect because you know that being present in the situation means being equal to it. You fully respond to what is happening versus what you wish were happening. You are breathing and can read the room. With this awareness, you make the most effective decisions based on the reality in each moment. You are listening and you're willing to offer your ideas and reach consensus with your fellow performers. A first circle improviser pulls energy from the group; a third circle improviser pushes too hard; a second circle improviser enlivens the room and invites connection. In second, you make others feel seen and heard. Second can be a calm, Zen state; however, an energized second circle is also a powerful physical state. Soccer players running downfield as fast as they can are in second together. Great athletes are often naturally in second. Take a moment to think of hobbies you may have that put you in the zone, that is, fully immersed in the present moment.

There is nothing wrong with first or third circles. They have their place. There are situations in life where you may need to shut down or take firm control to survive. If you are an introvert, you may use first circle to go inward and rejuvenate to gather your energy and reenter the world in second. For introverts, first circle can feel very comfortable, but it's essential to understand how that affects those around you and know you have a choice. It is not a giant leap to move from first to second. You adjust your posture, take a deep breath, make eye contact with the other performers, and make yourself open to the reality of the situation. Second circle is an invitation to everyone around you that you are ready to connect. Please note that you will not shift someone out of first by coming at them in third; this may push them deeper into first. If you are playing with someone in third, your only shot at connection will be to remain firmly in second yourself so that you can draw them toward you.

I want to add another layer to the foundation of second circle. The psychologist Harriet Lerner writes about "under- and overfunctioning" in her book *The Dance of Connection*. Under- or overfunctioning is a behavioral response to anxiety that we may develop during our early formative experiences.

If you're an underfunctioner, you become less competent under stress. You may freeze and want to be guided or rescued. Your thinking might sound like this:

"I'm confused."
"I can't help."
"They will judge me."
"Whatever I do will be wrong."

"I need help."
"I want this to be over."

Know that being confused or wanting to be rescued onstage can be a patterned response to anxiety. If you can sense what underfunctioning feels like in the body and know how to shift to second circle, you will connect better to others. It's critical to make the mind-body connection. Your thinking is what creates a physical state of helplessness: first circle.

In contrast, overfunctioners move quickly to rescue, give advice, or micromanage to control or overwhelm their anxiety. Their thinking might sound like this:

"I've got this."
"I will fix it."
"The others are incapable."
"I don't need help. I help."
"It's up to me—once again."

As an improviser, if you understand that wanting to control scenes is a patterned response to anxiety (third circle), you may redirect yourself in the moment and find second circle. In second, you will be able to read the room and know whether you should enter the scene or stay out. You will sense if you are trying to control the scene's direction or, instead, cocreate with your partners.

Under- and overfunctioning are armor protecting you from feeling vulnerable. These are simply patterned responses and not profound truths about who you are. You may realize sometimes you default to underfunctioning, and sometimes you default to overfunctioning. Take a moment to think about your default when you improvise—not in your best moments, but when you start feeling anxious or uncertain about what to do next.

Since 2005 I have been teaching second circle to the improv community. I have always identified with first circle or underfunctioning as my default when I'm not my best-balanced self in an improv show. However, when the COVID-19 pandemic hit in March 2020, my response to anxiety and the unknown was as follows: I applied for a business loan; refinanced our home; moved all of our in-person training to virtual classes; started training with a new company and helped put that program online; oversaw my website redesign; finished this book; reorganized my house thoroughly; wallpapered the guest bathroom and kitchen; and repainted a bathroom along with the inside of all of our closets and cabinets. Since I thought my husband was moving too slowly (he wasn't—this was just my anxiety), I also completed the tasks on his to-do list. So in real life I'm an overfunctioner. I relish bringing order to chaos, and when I look back over my life, many significant achievements are due to my overfunctioning. Yet when my husband compliments me on being strong and able to accomplish so much, instead of smiling and saying thank you, I either feel resentment bubble up or burst into tears. This reaction tells me how off balance I've been. Logically, I understand that being in second circle when under pressure will enable me to stay connected to those around me and collaborate. However, when real-life anxiety washes over me without awareness, I tend to default to the overfunctioner.

We all need to develop a calm practice to keep us from defaulting to patterned behavior that may not be the best for the situation. Brené

Brown, in her podcast "Unlocking Us with Brené Brown," defines calm as "perspective, mindfulness, and the ability to manage emotional reactivity." This definition also describes second circle. Calm people bring perspective to complicated situations. The feeling of calm is just as contagious as anxiety. When preparing to improvise with others, ask yourself, "Do I want to inject them with anxiety or calm?"

To improvise successfully, you want to be in second circle. You want to be aware of your habitual response to uncertainty, understand the thinking that pulls you into first and third, and know how to find and sustain second circle.

In narrative improv, you want to be conscious and aware of everything happening but not overthinking or over-trying. But how can you be consciously unconscious? A better way to describe it might be to say that you're so concentrated, so focused that your mind is still. Your mind becomes one with what your body is doing, and the unconscious automatic functions work without interference from thought. The concentrated mind has no room for thinking about how well a scene is going. In this state, there is little to interfere with the full intention to connect and create. This is the art of effortless concentration.

What disrupts this effortless concentration is that we have two selves inside each of us. You might have some awareness that you talk to yourself. I know I do. I am painfully aware that I speak to myself in my head: an ongoing, one-sided monologue gives me commands and comments on my actions. This part of myself will sometimes speak so loudly when I'm improvising that it's hard to hear or notice anything else. Let's call this part self 1. Self 1 tends to give instructions; its counterpart, self 2, performs the action. Then self 1 returns with an evaluation of the action. So the teller is self 1, and the doer is self 2.

The key to better improvising lies in improving the relationship between self 1, the conscious teller, and the natural capabilities of self 2. Self 2 includes the unconscious mind and nervous system that hears everything and never forgets anything. It knows what to do. That's its nature. However, self 1 doesn't trust self 2 to do its job even though self 2 embodies all the potential you have developed up to a given moment and is far more competent in carrying out physical actions than self 1. Self 1 thinks too hard and tries too hard, producing tension and muscle conflict in the body.

We don't want self 1 to lead while onstage. We, the audience, want to relax. Lead with self 2, staying in second circle. It's the constant thinking activity of self 1 that causes interference with the natural capabilities of self 2. Harmony between the two selves exists when your mind is quiet and focused.

If you trust self 2 and let it *be*, your narrative will flow easily. You want to feel your way through a story rather than think your way through. That's when you transport your audience with the story you are creating. It won't ever go perfectly, but letting your body lead (self 2) is vital to your success.

However, you can't just make self 1 stop talking. You need to give self 1 a job and a focus, and one of the most important ways to channel this focus is by creating the world of the play.

3

THE WORLD OF THE PLAY

No matter if you are watching a film, TV show, or play—or even reading a short story or novel—I can tell you one thing: it exists some*where*. There is a location or even multiple locations where the characters reside.

This is key for you to know when you improvise a scene or longer story. Establishing the where is not just a "nice to have," it's a *must* have. If you aren't anywhere specific, you and your fellow performers are just improvisers standing near each other and thinking or trying to be clever.

In second circle, your body, breath, and voice will come naturally, adapting to the evolving, long-form story you're telling. Now what do you do with your mind? Give it a job. Focus on creating a world to inhabit. This *where* will create characters with desires who will move your story forward. If I were teaching you how to play basketball before I gave you the game's rules, I would first show you, through repetition, basic actions like shooting, passing, and dribbling. Only then would it make sense for me to help you develop an intellectual understanding of the length of a game, where your basket is, and what is required to win the game. Before being thrown into a game, you must align the coordination system—your self 2—to take over when the game begins. That's what we focused on in chapter 2. This chapter focuses on the playing field, the court, and how to *be* on that field so you can play the game better.

In short, this chapter will give your second circle body and mind a focus that will activate your imagination. You will learn how to create the world with physical and verbal actions and endowments; place yourself in the most dynamic improvised blocking that will help tell the story; and see the stage and your fellow improvisers so that your story builds from what is present. Only then can you shift easily into creating characters that connect with the audience. The where, and the characters you create, will work together to form the narrative.

Creating the World

Where are you right now? Wherever you are is affecting your body whether you know it or not. An environment affects its inhabitants. When you improvise a full-length play, you must create a visceral environment that you both see in your mind and feel physically. This will transport you and the audience. In short-form improv, the environment work is often the weakest link. Improvisers run onstage and hastily do actions to let people know where they are, but it rarely feels fleshed out or real.

Think about what happens first when you attend a play or a movie. In a play, the lights go down and the curtain begins to rise. The set is slowly revealed. It is lit in a specific way to evoke a mood. The music you hear supports this. The genre dictates the look and sound; for example, it might be a moody noir with dramatic lighting and ominous music. When I do long-form, improvised, rom-coms, we ask the audience for the name of a city, a time of year, and an occupation. Our improvised opening scene combines these elements to create the opening location as well as introduce the story's lead character. Imagine what would happen without the elements of a specific location and time of year: the improvisers would go out onstage and just start talking, navigating back and forth until they found out the who, what, and where. Knowing *where* you are is a launching pad that mirrors what an opening of a movie or play does. It pulls viewers in immediately and gives you a structure to work within. The viewers don't have a lot of context yet, but we are somewhere specific so their minds are engaged.

Using words and actions to place images in your audience's mind helps to stimulate emotion and memory in yourself. How you relate physically to the environment creates character and story. There are improvised stories that I still see in my mind thirty years later. In one scene at BATS Improv in 1995, the audience location prompt was "a campsite." The stage lights dimmed, cricket sound effects played, and an improviser carefully pretended to light a fire in a pool of light. I can still remember the stage with a big campfire in the center. I see the silhouettes of trees surrounding the actor, who, in my mind, was wearing a thick jacket because of the cold and dark. Suddenly, a fellow improviser ran onto the stage yelling about sounds he had heard and went through a tree I had seen in my mind, stopping in the middle of the fire. This entrance was the moment I lost connection to the actor on the stage. The one who had created the fire sat and stared at what would have been the burning legs of his friend. But he didn't know how to justify it so he just looked where his friend was pointing.

There are so many things to unpack here. This was a "Hey, Kool-Aid" moment, but the first improviser could have started patting the flames on his friend's legs out, letting the second improviser know they were standing in a fire. What if this person had never entered the scene at all? I suspect that they entered because the scene was quiet and they didn't trust what was thus far the audience's muted reaction. This scene would have otherwise been a lovely reprieve from the raucous, short-form games that had comprised the evening so far. Before the second performer had come running in, we were transported into a location cocreated by the first improviser onstage and those managing the lights and sound. The imagination is powerful. There had been nothing else on the stage up to that point, yet I *still* see the details in my mind.

To further illustrate how a specific opening of *where* creates character and story, let's use the rom-com genre. Let's say suggestions from the audience start the story in a Chicago coffee shop during the winter. You thank them for the suggestion and clear the stage. As the lights go down, the music swells. After a brief moment, the members of the ensemble step onstage to fill out the where. What do we know so far? It's winter in Chicago, so it's cold. If I am a customer entering the scene, I wear lots of layers and am happy to have entered a warm place. I may have a hat, gloves, scarf, and a big jacket to attend to as the scene progresses. If I'm a customer in the cafe near the door, I may react whenever the door opens, and cold air rushes in. Maybe I keep my coat on because of this or look at the door with disgust whenever it's opened. Maybe I will try to move away from the door. My reaction to the door and how I respond could make me one of the leads in this improvised play.

If I work in this coffee shop in winter in Chicago, instead of being a customer, I have to deal with the unhappy customer sitting too close to the door. How I deal with this shows who I am as a character. In this scene, what is at stake for the lead and who they are as a person is revealed by everyone they interact with, but this opening location will be a touchstone for us to revisit throughout the play. If it's cold and winter and public in the first scene, we follow the lead home in the second scene. What a lovely contrast to be cozy, warm, quiet, and private there. We learn more about our lead by how their home environment looks and how they respond to it. If you have seen any Nancy Meyers or Nora Ephron rom-coms, you will know how important the home environment is to the lead character's development. Consider the home of Meg Ryan's character in *You've Got Mail* or Diane Keaton's in *Something's Gotta Give*.

As an improviser, you want to fully be in the scene's location, which will tell you what to say. You don't need to be in your head (self 1) thinking of what to say or controlling where this scene will go. If you lead with self 2, you are seeing and hearing everything. This observation makes you aware and quiets the mind. You will know what to do when you play from self 2, your second circle self.

Choosing a Location

There are a few different approaches to selecting a location for the play and getting the story underway.

1. Ask the audience for a specific location. Once you have the location prompted, envision it in your mind and begin the physical actions that convey what you are feeling in that space.

2. If you don't ask for a location, the first performer should have one in mind. They can verbally say something to provide the next improviser with clues or cue them with physical sculpting, such as standing downstage pretending to stare out a window, lounging on chairs as if they are a sofa, or laying face down on the floor. Alternatively, they may be vacuuming hurriedly, washing dishes angrily, or performing another action. Whatever it is, they should commit and be clear about what they're doing.

3. Let your tech improvisers on lights and sound set the mood and tone for you before you enter. Work in sync with your tech team.

Exercise: Connecting to a Space

Take a moment to check where you are right now and how you relate to your environment physically, mentally, and emotionally. You can either get up and be active in your space or stay seated and just look around you. It's important to note how it feels to you either way as you do the following.

- Sit or stand and breathe while cultivating a second circle mind-set. Look at or touch the *floor*. What materials are present? How does it feel underfoot?

- Now notice the *walls*. Are they smooth, cool, or warm?

- Look above you. What is the *height* of the ceiling overhead? Are there any details you haven't noticed before?

- Now note the *texture* in the room. Is there wood, metal, straw, glass or fabric?

- Now notice the *light and shadow* in your space. Take in where the light is coming from and note the shadows created. Is the light natural or human-made? How does it make you feel?
- Now take in *color* or lack of color in this space. Is there a predominant color? How does it make you feel?
- Last, take in the *sound* of your environment.
- Now close your eyes and try to feel the space you've just explored all at once. Add the room's temperature: cold, warm, hot, or just right? What time of day is it? Is your mind focused or scattered? Are you physically comfortable or not? Do you need to stretch or readjust? Is there a scent in the room that you are aware of? Are other people in the space? What are you noticing about them?
- Finally, come back and open your eyes, keeping your visceral connection to the room.

Working with Your Tech Team

The setting you create with your tech improvisers will add to the play you are creating on the spot. When I was working with Impro Theatre in Los Angeles we would have sets built for us that evoked the world of the play. It had to be specific to the genre, yet open to interpretation, as we were improvising a different story every night. What I love about working on sets is that there is furniture for you to respond to, doorways to enter, or downstage pools of light to monologue in. All of this helps create a visceral response for the improvisers and the audience.

Filling out a location creates a narrative, and this also changes depending on the genre. For example, if I'm doing a *passion noir* (black-and-white film from the 1940s to 1950s) and the starting location is a bedroom, I immediately picture a seedy studio apartment in downtown Los Angeles with a Murphy bed covered in rumpled sheets. This picture flashes in my mind, and then the character who inhabits it appears. If I started the scene, I would start with physical activity. I could be lounging on this bed, smoking, and reading a racing form. I could be pacing the floor anxiously waiting for a phone call or hurriedly packing. I don't know anything yet, but filling out the where and physically inhabiting it gives me emotion and the beginnings of the story.

If I'm in a rom-com and receive the suggestion of a bedroom, I might picture a room with a luxurious bed, perfect lighting, and my little dog asleep next to me as I read. The small detail of the book title I'm reading will say a lot about my character. For a buddy action film, if we ask the audience for the buddies' two opposing traits at the show's beginning, my adjective lets me know what my room looks like and what my reaction to the environment should be: messy, fastidious, impatient, long suffering, short fused, optimistic, fearful, and so on. Your imagination will freely give you images you can make physically real for yourself, your fellow improvisers, and your audience.

Dynamic Staging

The following contains my specific techniques for developing more dynamic staging, which entails taping the floor and conducting different exercises. I started taping the rehearsal floor when I became frustrated that improvisers kept standing in un-energized blocking on the stage unless the focus of the scene was good blocking. As a story progressed, actors would gravitate toward static, safe blocking that makes sense in real life but is dull on the stage. You want to train yourself to *feel* when it's right to move and face out so the audience can see your facial reactions. Improvisers are fortunate that they can improvise their blocking! Therefore every movement should come from an internal feeling and direction. I might quickly move to the window with my back to the door when someone I'm attracted to arrives. I may angle my body away from someone I don't trust. Body placement tells the story. The audience will believe what you *do* more than they'll believe what you *say*. Dynamic staging requires less talk and ignites the stage with energy.

Step One

- Place yourself downstage center.
- Put a blue *X* there with blue painter's tape.
- Turn around and take a big step away from the audience and put a blue *X* there with the tape. (I'm 5'7", and when I place the *X*s, they seem to work well for everyone. You don't want them to be too close or too far apart.)
- With your back to the audience, take another big step and put a blue *X* there. That's your center row.
- Add six more *X*s on either side of the line you've just created, giving you a 9 x 9-foot grid.

(Audience Here)

X X X

X X X

X X X

(Back of Stage Here)

Step Two

Place one actor on a blue *X*. Then ask the actor to move from one *X* to another, stopping them on various *X*s and asking the rest of the group what status or narrative beat each position suggests. Different postures at each position will imply different things: facing the audience on the center *X* is a different start of a scene than on an *X* in the back, crouched down and facing away. But even without the physical sculpting, *where* you are on the stage tells a story.

Next, add another actor on a different *X*, which will put the actors in relationship to each other. Ask the others how each arrangement changes the status of the characters and the story they are in.

The actors should begin experimenting with different positions and postures. I use the following rules: You can stand, sit, or lie down on an *X*. You can walk around the *X*s on the stage, but when you stop moving, you must be on an *X*. You can face forward, sideways, or backward on an *X*. Two people can chase each other, or be on one *X*.

Emotion and dynamic tension will naturally develop due to the constricted world in which the actors are working. As it develops, the emotional essence of the scene should dictate the actors' movements. Very often I have to coach from the side and encourage the actors to move around. One important rule is if an actor wants to move to the middle *X*, they must go via one of the corners. When I took this rule away, it removed some of the tension from the stage. If you have your performers stick to this rule, they may get cornered, and they may not get what they want—which is a perfect way to help them be adaptive!

Step Three

Invite two actors to place themselves on *X*s, taking note of where their partner is, and have them start a scene based on what kind of story their relative positions suggest. Have them do the entire scene on the *X*s, experimenting with moving or being still and observing what more dynamic movement does to the energy of the scene. If they keep settling into dull blocking, encourage them to be dynamic.

Step Four: Nonverbal Sculpting

Start with one person onstage. Have them randomly pick an emotion from an envelope full of different emotions listed on tiny pieces of paper. They should then select the *X* that feels right for that emotion and sculpt themselves to express this emotion. If I pick "proud," I might place myself on the center *X* standing up with face beaming. If I select "ashamed," I might get into a fetal position on the farthest *X* with my back to the audience.

Give the first person a few moments to marinate in their pose. Then have a second person enter, observe the first person, and respond only though body language. The two converse physically like this briefly before they start talking while continuing to use their body language. If my partner is in a fetal position way up in the far corner, I might curl up with them, and we'd start the scene from there. Or I might stand over them, or I might stand on the opposite *X* downstage facing the audience with my arms folded. Start physically with silence, and you will immediately sense the story.

Exercises like this encourage more interesting blocking and ensure your audience will feel the full impact of your story. Here are pictures from *The Portal: An Improvised Journey into the Unknown*, which took place over a series of streamed episodes. (You can see more pictures on imdb.com.) These improvisers improvised their blocking for the camera. They nailed it. You can too.

Sara Mountjoy Pepka and Arlo Sanders. PHOTO BY PAUL VONASEK. *THE PORTAL: AN IMPROVISED JOURNEY INTO THE UNKNOWN.*

Nick Clark, Stephen Kearin, Arlo Sanders, and Mike Rock. PHOTO BY PAUL VONASEK. *THE PORTAL: AN IMPROVISED JOURNEY INTO THE UNKNOWN.*

Kirsten Farrell, Jo McGinley, Nick Clark, and Kelly Lohman. PHOTO BY PAUL VONASEK. *THE PORTAL: AN IMPROVISED JOURNEY INTO THE UNKNOWN.*

Nick Massouh and Brian Jones. PHOTO BY PAUL VONASEK. *THE PORTAL: AN IMPROVISED JOURNEY INTO THE UNKNOWN.*

Other Exercises

Verbally Endow the Environment

This exercise will help improvisers describe a location by endowing the environment at the beginning of their improvised play.

33

Instructions

- Pair improvisers up and scatter them throughout the room.
- Each pair should pick one person who will start (person A).
- Person B will give person A a location to describe, which might be the setting of a made-up play—for example, a laundromat, a living room, the deck of a boat, or an attic.
- Set your timer for two minutes.
- Person A will describe the made-up environment as if persons A and B are in the environment. Encourage them to move around the location and touch the things they mention. Person A should speak quickly so they can bypass the impulse to overthink. They should go into great detail about what they see, which means they will not get to the whole environment in those two minutes but give a specific description of what has come up so far—not mentioning other characters or plot points, just the environment's endowments.
- At the end of two minutes, person B will prompt them to describe specific aspects of the environment that haven't been mentioned yet or those they want to hear more about. I suggest having these prompts written out. Set your timer for another two minutes. The prompts are
  - solid mass: What are the walls like in this space? Notice the floors. How do they feel underfoot? How high is the ceiling? Describe it.
  - texture: Is there texture in the room? Is it wood, metal, fabric? Describe and touch it.
  - light: Where are the light sources in the room? Are they natural or human-made? Where are the shadows?

- color: Is there a predominant color in the room? What colors are here?
- sound: What sounds do you hear in the room and outside the room?
- For the final minute, person B gets to ask for any details about the space just described that are still unclear in their imagination.
- Now switch. Person B guides person A in a *new* made-up space using the steps above.
- Debrief: At the end of the exercise, when both sides have gone (five minutes each), take time to ask the following.
  - What details remain in your mind about the locations described?
  - What type of people might inhabit the space you created?
  - What else strikes you as a valuable lesson from this exercise?

Inhabit the Environment

- Keep those same pairs together and have them do short scenes in the location they've just described. Without focusing too much on narrative, they should see what kinds of stories and emotions come from being in that specific place.
- Now have everyone sit down while keeping two new improvisers onstage. They should take thirty seconds each to describe a *new* environment together. They should then improvise a scene in this new location using dialogue to build the area even more. They will find that character and behavior, and therefore, the story will come out of taking their time to be in this place together.

Environmental Memory

Pair everyone up and ask one person in each pair to take the other person on a tour of their real childhood bedroom. For instance, if I were to describe for you my childhood room, I would say, "You stand at the door looking in, and on your left are posters of dogs and cats covering all the wall space available, wood-paneled closet doors, and a blue-and-green floral chair with stuffed animals and a terrifying, life-size Raggedy Andy doll. Above the chair is a window that looks out over the top of the pine trees on the property. The walls are painted sky blue, and the curtains and bedspread are bright white. The walls and this white make you think of the sky and clouds when you are in there." I would go on from here for the duration of time. Three minutes is sufficient, then you can switch.

Note: This is a powerful exercise. You will notice when people see a place in their mind and describe it, they naturally use gestures rather than just words. Have people move about the space as they are describing it so we get a sense of the orientation of the room and its size. Behave as if you are in the room you are describing and do what you would do to show it to someone.

Entrance Exercise

This exercise helps you practice entering a space as a way to *start* a scene. One at a time, your ensemble comes onto the stage, acting out how they walk in the door when they (as themselves—not a character) arrive home.

For example: I, Jo, am always slightly out of breath because my arms are full as I never want to make a second trip to the car and I'm struggling to find my keys. I always fall inward a bit and look to put some of my things down as I'm saying hello to my dog, who is at the top of the stairs wagging her tail, making tapping sounds with her toenails, and looking slightly concerned. I'm also trying to grab the mail dumped through the mail slot. It's ridiculous, but it's me, and I would try to replicate this feeling in rehearsal.

You want to have everyone do it the first time acting as themselves, which makes it much more visceral. As performers develop their ability to communicate through entrances, they'll be able to use them to help define characters. In the rom-com structure I teach, we see our lead arrive home in the second scene, and how the character enters their home tells us a lot about them quickly.

Virtual Inspiration

It became apparent for us very early in the COVID-19 pandemic that Zoom was a great virtual platform on which to create improvised stories. However, it did require each improviser to be able to move around their home and use different light sources. While I live edited the camera spotlight and underscored it with music, our creativity was stimulated. One class had people in Japan, Berlin, Manhattan, Los Angeles, Traverse City, Orlando, Atlanta, and Chicago. We were spread out but we were all connected in this one space improvising together online. It was incredibly inspiring.

Using a real environment added so much. I asked one student, Carla, to take me to her kitchen and she did a scene with someone else in *their* kitchen. The sounds of running water, the clang of dishes and the sounds of chopping vegetables added so much to the narrative of their scene. Instead of feeling stuck with a green screen, let this inspire you. You can bring this physical knowingness next time you are in a black box theater. Pay attention to how your body moves in space and let this part of you take over.

The ability to move around your space or change the angle of your cameras is beneficial for the following exercise in which the goal is to use the characteristics of the actual environment (based on the same prompts as above) to inspire the scene. After all, if you lean against a cold cement wall, that will give your character a point-of-view and emotions different from those that being curled up on a couch wrapped up in a cozy blanket would give.

Solid Mass: Try focusing your camera on a wall, then the floor, then the ceiling. Your camera may already be positioned with a wall as the backdrop; if not, choose to focus on one of the walls and step in to frame and start the scene. Then focus the camera on the floor and use what you see there to find the story. Then tilt your camera back to start the scene with only a view of the ceiling, with a performer entering the scene and looking down into the camera. Find the story from there.

Texture: Use one of the surface textures in the room as the starting point for the scene. Whatever it is, have it launch you and then find a story from there. (These scenes tend to feel like David Lynch wrote them.) Texture can be that of fabric, baskets, raffia wallpaper, a fur throw, and so forth.

Light and Shadow: Eliminate all the light in your room and then start with one light source to see what it gives you, for example, candles, a fire, lamplight, a flashlight, a computer light, a phone light, a spotlight. Scenes done with specific light, live editing, and added music feel like tiny little films. They can be gorgeous. When rehearsing over Zoom I would pair people up and send them to breakout rooms for two minutes to decide on what light sources they would use for their scenes. Then I would bring them back, and we would see these scenes. They didn't have time to plan a story, just a light source. I would spotlight their videos, and we would enter the worlds they created.

Sound: You can use sound effects played from your computer, or focus on what you can hear in your environment. What happens when listening to the environment is used as a launchpad to start the scene?

Go Outside

Rehearsing in a black box theater can feel stifling. In 2005 we were rehearsing in our studio when I felt that everyone, including me, needed to get outside. It was a lovely warm night in Los Feliz so we locked up the room and headed outdoors. The first location was a stairwell with rather noir-like shadows. I asked two improvisers to sculpt themselves in the location and start a scene. We, the audience, closed our eyes until they were set and told us to look. As soon as our eyes were open, the scene had begun. Everyone's physicality and clarity were expressive. We moved on and did scenes in every location that struck our fancy. When you look at the world this way, especially at night, it's like you're living on a set. Real life may interrupt your intense conversation, and so you quiet down as someone approaches or a loud siren forces you to stop speaking for a moment. When we only see what the camera, or light, wants us to see, what is possible?

I highly recommend leaving your studio and finding good outdoor settings. You might be surprised how many locations are appealing, especially at night. You can have your group pick a spot that inspires them. It's fun to see things through their eyes. Have them decide where their audience will stand and then ask the audience to close their eyes. Once the actors have sculpted themselves in the location, they tell the audience to open their eyes. It's magical to open your eyes and see the scene right there. It's as if you are suddenly in a film. Adding a stairwell's varying levels, an alley's depth of field, or the ambient sound of traffic and sirens can inspire incredible scenes. To see your students pause to stop speaking for a moment as people pass by is a real-life moment that we often don't see enough onstage. You can even layer genre onto the outside locations. I once saw a tremendous Shakespearean scene on the steps of a closed church and an intense noir scene in the doorway of an old bookstore.

Our class in Los Feliz ventures outside in search of noir locations.
PHOTO BY PAUL VONASEK.

Jill Hoffman and Paul Marchegiani, along with the shadow of Andrew Pearce, discover the story through setting. PHOTO BY PAUL VONASEK.

Continuing to work with those outdoor scenes once you are back inside is a great teaching tool. It helps to expand the mind around what's possible in a black box theater.

4

CREATING CHARACTERS
WE CARE ABOUT

In creating a character that an audience will want to spend two hours with, it's imperative to have an inner world that propels you through the narrative. It's also crucial to start physically, tapping into how this makes you feel before you layer on a want or need.

There are characters that I played twenty years ago that I still remember—where I have a sense of having spent a lot of time in their skin, and yet it was only for an improvised play that *one* night. I was once performing *Chekhov UnScripted* with Impro Theatre at the Broad Stage in Santa Monica. We were being directed by Dan O'Connor, and through his tutelage, I absolutely fell in love with Chekhov. (Read Chekhov's short stories!) To start our entirely improvised Chekhov play, we would ask the audience for a view to begin our improvised play. In this particular show, we were given "pond with ducks." As the stage was illuminated, I ran to the front window to see if I could spot the baby ducks that I had been told were born. I was full of energy and anticipation. In my mind, I was very young. Behind me the brilliant

Brian Lohmann endowed me as his excitable wife, and he and a fantastic fellow improviser Kelly Bashar talked in hushed tones about my fragile emotional state.

This fragility was an absolute gift. A neighbor (Stephen Kearin) came to call, and he had a cane with a duck head on it—not a mimed cane, but a real, actual cane that happened to have a duck's head. I became obsessed with him, the cane, the ducks, all of it. The narrative that evolved was that I had learned I could not bear a child, which I found unendurable. In the end, I was walked offstage past the pond, past the same window I had excitedly peered through at the beginning, by a very kind doctor as my husband, neighbor, and concerned sister-in-law watched me taken away.

Working with improvisers who will see and respond to your offers is a gift. If we all do that, our narrative will move forward effortlessly. This show had flawed characters who made you feel you were watching a play. If anyone of us had been locked in a short-form mindset, we wouldn't have created a riveting story together. Responding to the *where* will give you a point of view. You can express that perspective physically, emotionally, and verbally, and these together create character.

In the rehearsal process, keep expanding your character range. Do the following character exercises to help create characters that feel authentic to you, your fellow improvisers, and your audience.

It's in the Cards: Characters with a Point of View

I have created point-of-view (POV) cards for every genre I teach, and I have non-genre POV cards as well. I used them when my husband

Stephen and I directed our 2013 *Twilight Zone UnScripted* at the Garry Marshall Theatre in Toluca Lake, California. We were practicing episode starts, and my scene partner and I took a card from an envelope I had filled with POVs that were appropriate for 1950s America and the themes of Rod Serling's *Twilight Zone.* My scene partner started the scene as a little boy with a lemonade stand and sweetly called me "Mrs. Wilson" when our scene began. My card had read, "I'm suspicious of you," so I became a very wary neighbor who didn't trust this little boy's intentions. What was he *really* about? Who was he actually? It was ridiculous and fun and right in the emotional universe of McCarthyite America in the 1950s. If I hadn't picked this card, I would not have done the scene this way, and it stands out as one of my favorites. POV cards are a great way to shake up your routine and expand your range.

Playing a character with a clear point of view energizes the stage. When your scene begins, there is no time to overthink your reaction to it. In the Chekhov duck scene, all I knew at the start was that I felt joy and couldn't wait to see the baby ducks. I didn't know where the scene would go—that was none of my business. I just saw the window, the pond, and the sunny skies and trusted the process.

A POV is a filter through which everything your fellow performers offer passes. With practice, you will know when to maintain your POV and when to let it change. For example, in our approach to the buddy action genre, the characters' feelings about each other and their worldviews are altered over the course of the story. In the *Twilight Zone* genre, we know to give a character their comeuppance if they don't change when given a chance. In rom-coms, a character's fear-driven life map may hinder their finding or accepting love: their first circle tendencies may keep them siloed, but we want to see if they work through this and change. The story will unfold organically, moment by moment, from your character's behavior and desires.

There is a more comprehensive list of POVs in the exercises section below, but first take a moment to think how different your characters would be with these varied POVs.

About Yourself

- "I'm at the end of my rope."
- "I must be content with my lot in life."
- "I'm the center of everything."
- "I would love an exciting life!"
- "I need everything to be perfect."
- "I was glorious once."

About Your Scene Partner

- "I adore you."
- "I am suspicious of your motives."
- "I fear you're losing your mind."
- "You are my salvation."
- "You think I'm boring."
- "I love you, and you don't know."

Having an Objective or Want

You should have a POV about everyone onstage, and you should let the audience and the other performers see or hear that POV. Having a clear POV not only affects you physically and emotionally, it can lead you toward an objective. In improvised scene work, objectives are most valuable when connected to a want or a need that affects scene partners. In this way we observe characters trying to achieve their goal and watch how they are affected by whether their partner gives them what they want. The improviser might need to change tactics to achieve their objective, and whether they have succeeded will be clear.

There is a difference between blocking an improviser and blocking a want. Blocking an improviser—explicitly or implicitly saying no to an idea they've introduced to the story—stops a scene cold. By blocking a want, however, you have upped the stakes for the other character to achieve their goal. They must now take more risks or find a new way to achieve their objective. In blocking what their character wants, you have created more opportunities for story development.

In 2019 I embarked upon a fascinating journey with Impro Theatre. Matthew Pitner and Paul Hungerford had introduced the idea of streaming narrative improv on *Twitch TV*. Paul Vonasek, Nick Massouh, and I had been intrigued by the concept of telling stories via live television, like the 1950s TV show *Playhouse 90*. This all came together when we realized we could take my improvised version of *The Twilight Zone* and present it as a live televised version called *The Portal*.

This one-hour show consisted of three entirely improvised episodes in the style of Rod Serling's *The Twilight Zone*. One of our "asks" at the beginning of an episode was for an occupation that would have existed in the 1950s or 1960s. For this episode, we took "beautician." The lights went down, a *Twi-like* theme song played, and based on where we were standing when the lights came up, I realized I was the beautician.

Fellow improviser Edi Patterson had the first line.

Edi: Oh Linda, you are so good.

Me: That's what I've been trained to be, good.

    [I was wondering to myself, Am I an android?]

Edi: You're a wizard!

    [I wondered, So I have magic powers?]

    [I looked into the mirror and smiled. Then Kirsten Farrell spoke, playing a customer named Jackie.]

Jackie: I've been cutting my own hair.

Edi: Oh Jackie, don't get Linda angry.

Jackie: Linda, can you get me a mirror?

At that point I was at an improv crossroads. I'd been clearly looking into the mirror as I worked on Edi's hair. Could I not see myself? In the moment I didn't realize Jackie might have meant a hand mirror. Should I ignore this or mention it? I mentioned it.

    Me, pointing to the mirror in front of us: You can't see yourselves? I've been looking in that mirror all day.

After a beat, they got very angry with me, which led to a back-and-forth that escalated.

I won't go into the entire episode here, but it turned out the other two women were psychic vampires in my mind and my journey was about attaining a full acceptance of myself—of who I was as a person, a person who had to accept getting older. By the end of the episode I had accepted all of me, and they melted away. Leading up to that, though, I had to say no over and over again as they tried to get me to hate myself and embrace a negative self-perception. This was an instance of saying no in the service of a bigger yes.

Mike Rock's amazing improvised narration at the end went like this:

> This little light of mine, I'm gonna let it shine . . . It's been said that in order to see beauty in the world, one needs to see beauty in themselves. So, instead of looking outward, direct yourself inside and watch that mirror to find what's truly beautiful in yourself and in—*The Twilight Zone*.

Our *Twilight Zone* episode featured "psychic vampires" Edi Patterson (left) and Kirsten Farrell (right) inhabiting my mind. PHOTO BY PAUL VONASEK.

Remember that you speak to impact your scene partners. When you speak with purpose, the scene will be better defined than if you speak only to define the who, what, and where of the scene.

Sample Objectives

- to encourage
- to trick
- to confuse
- to destroy
- to defend
- to confess
- to beg
- to help
- to impress
- to entice
- to convince
- to flatter

Take a moment to think about what different types of characters come out of you depending on the character's objective. If I know I want to flatter you, that creates a different voice and physicality than if my objective is to destroy you.

Exercises to Develop Characters We Care About

POV Cards

This exercise forces you to try out different answers to such important character questions as Who is it I'm talking to? Why am I talking to this person? What is my attitude (POV) at the point I enter the scene? How do I feel about myself? My situation? The world at large?

Write the phrases below on separate index cards and have two performers each pick a card from the stack before they start their scene.
Once they've read their POV card, have them return the card to the
deck without sharing it with anyone and proceed to the stage, where
they will sculpt their physical posture, breathe, take in their partner's
physicality, and begin the scene.

About Yourself

- "I'm at the end of my rope."
- "I must be content with my lot in life."
- "I'm the center of everything."
- "I need to be worshipped and adored."
- "I would love an exciting life."
- "I need everything to be perfect."
- "I do what I'm asked."
- "I enthusiastically agree with everything that is said and done."
- "I uphold the rules."
- "I was glorious once."
- "I'm not like them; give me a chance."
- "Everything revolves around me."
- "I'm jealous."
- "I'm here!"
- "I inhale life."
- "I never say the right thing."
- "Sixty days clean and sober."
- "I'm dying. I'm sure of it."
- "I'm broke, embarrassed about it, and very lonely."

About Your Scene Partner

- "I adore you."
- "I'm suspicious of your motives."
- "I fear you're losing your mind."
- "We all need each other."
- "You don't know what it's like to be me."
- "I must please you!"
- "You are my salvation."
- "You're different from the others."
- "This will be our best year yet."
- "I'm embarrassed for you to see me."
- "I just want what's best for you."
- "You think I'm boring."
- "I forgive you."
- "I'm hurt you forgot my birthday." (With this POV, don't say it directly to the other performer too early in the scene.)
- "I fear you've joined a cult." (Likewise, don't say this directly too soon.)
- "I sincerely adore you."
- "I physically float around you."
- "I believe you are spreading rumors about me."
- "When are you going to admit you are in love with me?"
- "You remind me of my favorite pet."
- "We have everything in common!"
- "I cannot understand you." (You almost hear gibberish when they speak.)
- "What do you mean by that?" (You take offense at every offer from the other performer.)

- "I've read your diary."
- "I love you, and you don't know."
- "You are dying soon."
- "They are coming for us."
- "They are coming for you."
- "I think you are mentally ill, and I want to help." (Be as subtle as you can with this.)

About Your Location

- "This used to be such a pretty town."
- "I've had enough of this town forever."
- "I would give anything to go back there."
- "Everyone, everything seems so familiar."

Specific Behavior

- You can only say one word in this scene and may say it only once.
- You are subtly looking for a way to escape.
- You are desperate to get information about what happened the night of the accident—but you can't ask directly.
- You will ask the other performer to marry you at some point in the scene.
- You fill the room with your voice and constantly repeat your partner's character's name in various ways.
- You make references to animals throughout the scene.
- You start every sentence with "Remember when . . ."
- You mirror and copy what your partner says and does.

- You mimic your partner's energy, tone, and movements.
- You mimic your partner's style of speech: speed, tone, volume.
- You don't say anything about it and just respond physically when your mustache keeps sliding off.
- You believe you have invisible pigtails.
- You keep hiding your hands.
- You raise your arms when your partner is not looking at you and then lower them as soon as they look at you.
- You physically respond to your partner's voice because it hurts your ears.
- You tell your partner, "Physically looking up at you comforts me."
- You do not smile the entire scene. (This is great for chronic smilers.)
- You behave as though you're afraid you have bad breath. (Don't actually talk about it.)
- You behave as though you have a metal rod in your spine. (Likewise, don't actually talk about it.)
- You always have your hand on your head or shoulder.
- You touch everything with your cheek.
- You place your hands on your hips every time you finish a sentence and say, "Hmmm!"
- You stretch out the pauses before you speak. Every time.
- You make all of your movements ballet like. (Don't actually do ballet. Just have fluid, graceful movement.)
- You respond to a constant ringing in your ears.
- You imagine that on top of your head is a marble and if you move your head just right, the marble will go down a hole.

- You are continually trying to get something from between your front teeth.
- You sense that gravity has pulled your face down.
- You believe a laser beam of light figuratively comes out of your chest.
- You touch both your elbows always.

Objective Cards

This exercise presents performers with different emotional outcomes they must try to achieve in another performer. It also uses index cards, each of which has one of the objectives from the list below.

urge	guide	confound
quash	insult	comfort
confess	plead	claim position
incite	stun	probe
awaken	order	dazzle
defend	avoid	realize dream
push	resist	blast
stir	taunt	humor
caution	get attention	goad
rouse	save	derail
thrill	frighten	have fun
escape	not be alone	reflect
embolden	love	let go
object	pry	threaten
connect	shame	dismiss

- nail
- embarrass
- defy
- hide
- deflate
- hurt
- change
- tease
- lead
- delight
- confront
- repel
- demand
- cover guilt
- criticize
- implore
- respond
- protest
- face up
- mock
- beg

- seek consolation
- serve with love
- alarm
- provoke
- demand recognition
- delay
- compromise
- pull self together
- placate
- attack
- encourage
- relax
- admonish
- make life better
- praise
- impassion
- admit feelings
- repulse
- shock

- impress
- torment
- cajole
- devastate
- impress
- mystify
- bewitch
- intrigue
- terrify
- please
- protect
- appeal
- tempt
- reassure
- exalt
- allure
- pacify
- flatter
- inspire
- encourage
- irritate

Now pair actors up around the room. Each pair picks one card from the stack, and both read it. Actor A speaks lines of dialogue to actor B, one at a time, while actor B holds their hand in the air. Actor B can only lower their hand when actor A has achieved their objective, and actor A has three sentences at most to get their partner's hand down. If that hand is still in the air after three sentences, actor A asks actor B, "What do you need from me in order to put your hand down?" Actor B tells them, and then they can try again. This peer feedback is invaluable. Often you hear things like "Your tone doesn't match your words," or "You were using so many words I got lost," or "Just try it again with more conviction."

Sculpting and Positioning with POVs

This exercise takes place on a 9 x 9-foot grid (see chapter 3).

- Choose two performers and give each one a POV card.
- Direct them to choose an *X* to stand on and sculpt their body (see nonverbal sculpting, chapter 3) as inspired by the POV on their card.
- Beginning improvisers may choose to position themselves at a comfortable distance from their partner whether their POV calls for distance or not.
- The performers begin their scene, focusing on what positioning best conveys their POV. (An actor should always be aware of where their partner is and place themself accordingly.)
- Effective positioning might look like this: If my POV card says, "I am the greatest," I might place myself on the center *X*. If it says, "I can't think about this anymore," I might set myself face down across several *X*s. If it says, "I adore you," I will pay close attention to where my partner stands and place myself accordingly.

- If starting both actors with POV cards seems too much, you can always start by giving only one actor a card.

Sculpting the Other Performer

In this exercise, performers sculpt one another based on a specific emotion. The point is not for the sculpted performer to guess what the emotion is but to see how much their body posture informs their approach to the scene.

- Have everyone stand in pairs around the room and decide who will go first.
- The person who goes first picks an emotion on their own or from an envelope of emotions (see chapter 3).
- Without revealing the emotion to their partner, they begin sculpting their partner by directing them how to sit or stand and then moving their limbs into whatever shape best depicts their chosen emotion. (Note: Only touch with the other person's permission. They can also move their limbs on their own if you tell them what to do.) The goal is to create a sculpture of this emotion, as if for a museum.
- The person sculpted will marinate in this formation until they feel prompted to start a scene from this emotional place.
- When appropriate, the sculptor joins the scene, and both performers improvise together to the conclusion of the scene.
- Following this, they switch roles.

Finding Characters through Props and Furniture

I don't recommend using props when improvising. If you use mimed objects, you have everything you need at your fingertips. However, in the rehearsal process, using props and furniture can help you find characters inside you that you didn't know existed.

Many years ago, I was in rehearsal with fellow improvisers, and we combined the sculpt-your-partner exercise with props. My friend Kristina put a phone up to my right ear and made me stand over my friend Nick, pointing down to his foot with my left hand. Nick was sitting on a chair, hands folded, looking up at me sheepishly. In real life when I talk on the phone, I *always* put the phone to my left ear. My head tilts to the left as I speak. The simple act of someone placing an actual phone to my *right* ear completely changed my personality. This person who spoke on the phone with no head tilt to the left was the most believably aggressive character I've ever played. With my head straightened by a mere 2–3 inches, I was ripping the other person on the phone apart as the scene began. I had to justify why I was so angry and pointing to Nick's feet, so it turned out I was a PR woman who had been sent a model whose feet were too big for the shoes we were photographing. I still see Nick looking up at me so sweetly, blinking and shrinking, slowly curling his toes under to make his feet smaller.

Try this for yourself: Pair two performers, and then have two others pick a prop for each of them to use and sculpt them into position. It's not about doing weird things with props. It's about the actors learning how they behave in relation to real objects. What new points of view or characters can they explore this way?

Laban Movement Analysis and Power Centers

Rudolf Laban is considered one of the pioneers of modern European dance. He was a dance theorist and teacher, and his studies of human motion provided the intellectual foundations for Central European modern dance. Laban movement analysis (LMA) is a method and language for describing, visualizing, interpreting, and documenting all varieties of human movement. LMA is worth exploring in its entirety, but here I focus on the concept of *effort* for our improv acting purposes. Effort concerns both inner intention and how a movement is done. I may lift my arm to hit someone in anger, or I may lift my arm to reach for a glass of water. Both rely on extending my arm, but the effort differs.

Laban believed that several categories could classify different efforts and summarize human movement. Each effort is characterized in terms of space (how direct or indirect the movement is in moving from one point to another); time (how quick or sustained the movement is); weight (how heavy or light the movement is, i.e., how much force it carries); and flow (how bound or free the movement is). If you look at flow, a movement is bound when it's very tight and precise, like that of a stressed business person. If a movement flows freely, it is more impulsive or spontaneous, which may be more helpful in creating a childlike character.

The four categories of LMA define the eight efforts: *punch, skate, press, glide, thump, flick, plod,* and *float.* We can think of these in terms of the effort classifications above. You can add "bound" or "free" after direct or indirect in the list below.

punch: *fast, heavy, direct*
skate: *fast, light, direct*

press: *slow, heavy, direct*

glide: *slow, light, direct*

thump: *fast, heavy, indirect*

flick: *fast, light, indirect*

plod: *slow, heavy, indirect*

float: *slow, light, indirect*

Another important concept—one not taken from LMA—is that of the power center, the part of the body a performer leads with. Power centers can provide an excellent way for an actor to create a brand-new character by leading with a different body part. When I teach classes, based on what I know about each improviser, I will assign them a power center they normally don't use. It could be their chin, hands, hips, eyes, feet, and so forth. Jack Lemmon discussed using the top of his head as his power center in the movie *Missing*. To feel the tension there, he wore a hat a bit too small for his head. At a pivotal point in the film when his character breaks down, he removes his hat and pleads for help finding his son. So the too-small hat was the metaphorical lid he kept on his pent-up emotions until they exploded at that pivotal moment in the film. In an improvised scene, the intentional use of a power center can function as your touchstone: something you can keep coming back to that will anchor you to your character's point of view, emotional state, and physicality.

The following exercise combines LMA effort and power center concepts to help performers explore different approaches to developing a character.

- Have the actors onstage walking in second circle.
- Read the following script to them. The actors should not be looking at each other but moving around the room as the script directs them.

Start moving fast around the room. Be careful with each other, but move fast. Now make your movement heavy, too, so you are moving fast and heavy. Where are you going? What might you do for a living? [They don't need to say anything. You are just prompting them.] Now make your movement direct. Go where you intend to go. You are fast, heavy, and direct. The Laban effort term for this is *thrust*. Who might you be? What is the situation? Go ahead and keep moving while you say this out loud.

At this point you might hear "construction worker late for work," or "Wall Street trader on the floor," or "mother frantically looking for her child," for example. Allow enough time for each performer to identify their situation and encourage those who have been silent to say something. They might be stuck trying to find the right idea. Encourage them to say whatever they are feeling, not what they are thinking. Continue with:

Now, shake that off and go back to your neutral walk. Slow down, way down, and move much more slowly than you are now. Add lightness to your movement. You are moving slow and light. Where are you? What age are you? What might you be doing? Make your movement indirect. You are moving slow, light, and indirect. The Laban effort term for this is *float*. Where are you? What do you do for a living?

- Go through at least two more Laban efforts using similar scripts.
- Then bring in power centers with the following script.

> Start milling about the room again. Your power center is your forehead. Your forehead leads you through life. It's the first thing we notice when we see you. Commit to this 100 percent so you feel different than you normally do. Notice how different Laban efforts feel through your power center: fast or slow, heavy or light, and direct or indirect. Keep walking with the forehead leading the way. Who are you? Where are you going? What might you do for a living?

Using LMA and Power Centers as a Scene Start

The following exercise forces improvisers to make a physical choice, discover what story it gives them, and respond to a scene partner's offer with similar or contrasting physical choices.

- Have one person decide on specific Laban movements or a power center.
- Give the performer time to feel it in their body and use that to begin the story. For example, I'm moving fast, light, and direct and it makes me feel like I'm looking for something. I realize it's my keys.

- Another performer enters the scene. They can either join the first performer with the same type of movement (e.g., fast, light, and direct movement to help the first person find the keys) or they can do the opposite (e.g., slow, heavy, indirect) and see how that affects the story.

Eyes as an Offer

Eyes can be very important in defining character and POV. Have improvisers try the following eye placements and note how it makes them and their partners respond emotionally or physically. These can be used as a scene start or as a body awareness exercise.

- eyes cast downward
- eyes darting back and forth
- eyes looking upward
- eyes sustaining contact
- eyes avoiding contact

Animals: Another Way to Find a Character

One effective way to tie Laban, power center, and POV approaches is to pick an animal and let it inspire your character. For example, if I chose an elephant, I might think something like this.

- Laban: slow, heavy, direct
- power center: long trunk, swinging head
- POV: "I'm everybody's mama" or "I'll protect you."

Improvise a scene in which you are playing humans yet with each performer taking on one quality of an animal they have picked from a list of animals. My energy as an elephant-waitress will have very different Laban, power center, and POV characteristics than those of a hawk-waitress or a dog-waitress. Some particularly useful animals include

alligators	falcons	porcupines
ants	foxes	possums
armadillos	frogs	rabbits
badgers	gazelles	raccoons
bats	geese	ravens
bears	hawks	seahorses
beavers	horses	sharks
bees	hummingbirds	skunks
butterflies	lions	snakes
cheetahs	lizards	spiders
coyotes	moose	squirrels
cranes	mice	swans
crows	otters	tigers
deer	owls	turtles
dogs	oxen	weasels
dolphins	panthers	whales
eagles	peacocks	wolves

Early in the COVID-19 pandemic when classes were virtual only, there was a lot of innovative work to discover. I had students use their homes as sets and their cameras as creatively as possible. So much story came from what their camera revealed.

In one class, a student, Mimi, had set her camera on a wide angle. I pinned her video and her partner's as well so it was like calling two people to the stage. In the chat, I sent them each a private message with their animal from the list above. When two performers are assigned different animals, I never know how the pairings will work out, and it's exciting to see what unfolds.

Mimi walked deep into the frame into a corner and spread her arms out wide. She pawed at the walls with her arms outstretched and after a while began wailing in Japanese. There was so much grief and sorrow that we all sat very still and respectful. The animal she had been given was a spider, and she discovered that the physical action of holding her arms outstretched felt like grief. She crumpled to the ground at one point. Her partner, whose animal was an otter, came close to their camera and looked very kind, and concerned, with eyes blinking and attentive.

This was a beautiful example of finding story from specific physicality and relating to your environment. The scene stays with me to this day.

Improvising Monologues

The audience is the one with whom you, as a character, should always feel you can trust to share your innermost thoughts. You share your problems, wants, needs, and dreams with the audience. They get to know and love you because you reveal yourself to them, and improvised monologues are a great way to do that. Below I'll cover five different types of monologues.

Want Monologues

This is one of my favorite exercises as a teacher.

- Pair everyone in the room. Decide who in each pair is going first.
- Ask them to start a sixty-second monologue that begins with "I want . . ."
- Instead of reciting a laundry list of wants, performers should try to go into the *why* of their first articulated want. The first sentence states the want aloud, the subsequent sentences further develop the why behind the original want.
- Once time is up, have them switch roles and then provide feedback to one another.

The want monologue is a foundation for all genres. It's very helpful to have improvisers state aloud what they want or how they feel—anything to put themselves out there so they and the other performers have something to explore together. You can use this exercise as a warm-up drill at the beginning of every class or rehearsal. It can also be done with an environmental description incorporated.

- Pair everyone up in the room.
- Ask one person to go first and start a monologue with "I want . . ."
- After 30–40 seconds, call time.

- Now the performer who was giving the monologue will take the second performer on a tour of the home of the character they just started exploring through the improvised want monologue. Based on what they know so far, what kind of place is it? What does it look like? What specific items are in there that have meaning for our lead?

- Once the description is done, after about three minutes, the second performer will do a scene with the first one, establishing the situation with a line such as "As your roommate, I have to say . . ." The second performer must build on all the information the first performer has provided so far. It might be tempting to change or ignore some of it for a quick laugh, but if they remember they are there to flesh out the other character and the situation, everyone in the story will benefit.

- Have the two performers switch roles and run the exercise again.

Wonder Monologue

- Pair everyone around the room.
- One performer goes first and shares a description of a moment of genuine wonder from their life. It can be anything that comes to mind. They should be encouraged to be as descriptive as possible about how they felt in this moment of awe.
- The description might be short, and their partner can ask questions to help flesh the memory out. They switch roles once the description feels complete.

- Have the pairs debrief one another: What physical responses did you or your partner have when recalling a memory you saw in your mind? What kinds of human behaviors do you exhibit when you are telling a true story? The performers should remember and incorporate these behaviors over the next steps.

- One of the performers should then make up a story about a moment of wonder. Their partner can give them a prompt: Grand Canyon, cruise, sunset, favorite birthday, and so forth. Then the other performer does the same.

- The performers should provide feedback to one another, noting what physical responses and behaviors they see when they are improvising and if the story feels true.

Talisman Monologue

- Give the improviser an imaginary object to pretend to hold in their hands while standing in a pool of light and facing the audience downstage.

- Ask them to do a 1–3 minute monologue on why this object is vital to their character. Regardless of what it is—pen, snow-globe, lighter—their job is to make the object important and explain why. In their monologue, they should refer to the object itself while seeing it, describing it, and feeling its weight in their hands.

- You can also start with real objects by asking performers to bring something meaningful from home. This will allow you to discuss what behaviors manifest when an item that means something to them is actually in their hands. These behaviors and actions can then be applied to an improvised object.

- This monologue style is perfect for the villain in a buddy action story.

Why-I'm-Like-This Monologue

In the buddy action genre, the why-I'm-like-this monologue often occurs during a stakeout or other dramatic lull or in a moment of frustration when one of the cops asks the other to explain why they are the way they are. This launches a monologue that explains character and draws the other person closer to understanding.

- Pair performers around the room.
- Partner A gives partner B a character trait such as hotheaded, peaceful, jumpy, resigned, and so on. Partner B will then launch into their why-I'm-like-this monologue—that is, what events or experiences helped to make them this way.
- Once they reveal why they are hot-headed, for example, have them layer in a want. Their want is what would propel them through a full buddy action story.
- Good examples from films include Danny Glover in *Lethal Weapon*, who just wants to make it to retirement; and in *Midnight Run*, Robert DeNiro's character, who wants to get back to see his daughter.
- This monologue style is perfect for the buddies in the Buddy Action genre.

*You-Remind-Me-of-an-Animal [or Something-Else-from-Nature]
Monologue*

This exercise came from Brian Lohmann when Impro Theatre was rehearsing our show *Tennessee Williams UnScripted*. It works perfectly with many genres. You can do this as a small group or pair partners up around the room.

- Person A gives person B an animal or something from nature. Person B improvises a one-minute monologue talking directly to person A and explaining why person A reminds them of the animal prompted. For example, if the prompt was "mouse," person B might say:

  "You remind me of a little mouse. The kind of mice we have in this old house—ever-present yet unseen. There you go scurrying about in the shadows, observing us yet hiding your true self. What would it take to make yourself seen, little mouse? You have every right to be here; in fact, you've been here longer than me. Don't make yourself so small, mouse. You can't go on playing small to protect yourself. No one's going to hurt you, little mouse."

- Person A nods and listens, taking on the endowments from person B silently.

You can then have the mouse (person A) improvise a monologue back—maybe a why-I'm-like-this monologue. Or if the performers are in pairs, they can also just switch roles, with person B giving person A a prompt.

Let's continue from here to focus on key elements required to create compelling, improvised scenes.

5

CREATING SCENES THAT SPARK

Listening to the body benefits the improviser working onstage without a script. This ability has been dubbed *focusing* by the American psychotherapist Eugene Gendlin. Successful improvisers stop talking for a moment when they need to better pay attention to something inside themselves.

Gendlin called this hazy shadow, which a performer attends to and slowly allows to come to fruition, a *felt sense*. The felt sense is an inner ground from which thoughts, images, and feelings emerge when given time and attention. Sometimes improvisers lack the patience to allow this felt sense to take root and unfold. Instead, in their haste to give an answer for their discomfort with silence, they miss the opportunity for an organic response.

Gendlin discovered that the felt sense forms not in the head but in the body's center, somewhere between the throat and the stomach. The awareness of this sense is physical, and once it has been formed, heard, and accurately captured in a phrase or an image, there follows a corresponding physical sense of release and relaxation. It is as if some inarticulate part of the person feels, understands, and responds with a sigh of relief, "Yes. That's exactly how it is. You understand. Thank you." When this felt shift happens, the blocked feeling eases.

Take time in improv rehearsals or classes to receive a prompt and go inward to discover the felt sense, the answer to the question, "What is this whole thing about?" The usual default mode in improv is to leap to conclusions and construct a straightforward and plausible narrative as quickly as possible. But the felt sense (your self 2 from chapter 2) is wiser than our intellect—it gathers all the things we sense about the space we are in and the improvised story that's coming into being. But we can access it only if we let the felt sense form internally. This process may feel way too slow at first. It will become quicker as you practice improvising from the felt sense rather than the brain.

When you improvise a play, periodically rehearse in a way that allows plenty of time to engage with this felt sense. Silence is a gift. Allow time for the lines to land. Permit yourselves as improvisers not to know what to say next. Not knowing feels like real life. In real life, we can be caught off-guard and not know what to do or say, and seeing this onstage helps us recognize real-life moments.

We know from experience that improvisers tend to speed up when there is an audience. Some genres and types of scenes require quick responses so that pace and energy feel appropriate to the type of story. Train yourself to be an improviser who can be comfortable in a comedic, heartfelt, or tense scene. Be open and malleable to wherever your improvised theater takes you.

A study conducted by Princeton University researcher Uri Hasson examined the brain activity of storytellers and story listeners. It found that storytelling synchronizes the brain activity of both teller and the listener. While you are looping with your fellow improvisers, your audience is looping with you as well. "Your brain responses while listening become coupled to my brain responses, and slowly they become more similar to my brain responses," according to Hasson.[1]

The exercises I describe below, which help improvisers to slow down and engage with one another and their own felt sense, can work for various genres. Sometimes these have been the funniest scenes I've ever seen. Sometimes they are serious. You never know. I created this exercise to encourage neurological looping and help performers internalize information and offers from other improvisers so they can integrate them into their felt sense. Our brains are wired to connect with one mind at a time. How lovely to remove all the distractions and connect directly and deliberately with your scene partner, one line at a time! If you can achieve this connection, the effect can be riveting and pull an audience in.

Some improvisers find slowing down a relief or exciting, while others struggle. If you find you're struggling, stop to consider why it's a challenge. Not getting laughs might be making you feel vulnerable. Or you may be doubting your acting skills and are putting pressure on yourself to be good. A slower pace can be a relief for introverts or first circle improvisers as there is a limit to how long their partner can keep talking.

If your ensemble can create individual scenes that are compelling, we will want to watch a longer narrative. Become adept at creating rich scenes then add another scene, another, and another until you are improvising a one- or two-hour narrative, scene by scene.

So, So Scenes

I created this exercise by taking something from an acting class and knitting it into a narrative improv class. *So, So Scenes* allow the actors to feel what it's like to slow down, trust their partner will not talk indefinitely, take in what they say, and pick up on the nuances of their vocal tone or body language. The lines are linked, one after the other. The narrative that comes out of this exercise feels authentic and exciting because we see the origin of each moment. Inauthentic responses and forced emotions don't work here. By returning to this exercise often, your group will understand why slowing down and responding to the last thing said or done is invaluable to narrative improv. Let yourselves experience how gorgeous silence can be.

- Place two chairs in front of the group. The chairs should face and be close to each other but the actors' knees should not touch.
- Invite two actors to sit in the chairs, close their eyes, and focus on inhabiting second circle.
- When their eyes are closed, let them know who will go first (person A) and second (person B).
- Instruct them to open their eyes, breathe, take in their partner, and let that affect how they say the word *So*.
- Once their eyes are open, the scene has begun. Their job is to look into their partner's eyes and read them for intent and emotion. After they take each other in, person A says, "So."
- Person B listens to *how* their partner says *So* and reads their body language and then responds with their own *So*.

- From here on, they will take turns adding one line each turn. They should make statements, not ask questions. Remind them that they are not playing themselves: their character and the narrative will evolve as the scene unfolds with each of them responding to their partner's previous line. They need to respond to the truth of what they *hear and feel*, not what they *think*.

- From the outside, you will sense when they allow a line to land and respond to it organically. They may need to be encouraged to slow down and give the lines time to land. Let them know you will side coach if needed.

Example

A: (Opens eyes, takes in their partner, reads them for emotion.) "So?"

B: (Hears how A said "So" and responds accordingly) "So."

A: "You look anxious."

B: "I am because we haven't seen each other in a while."

A: "True."

B: "I was worried you were mad at me."

A: "I am."

B: "I've come to make amends."

A: "I'm listening."

    . . .

You can go on until the scene comes to a natural conclusion, or you call time. Improvisers should be encouraged to accept any label their partners assign them, reminding them that it's coming from what their partner has read in their eyes or body language. So, "You look anxious" must be a true response to something they see there. Performers will more quickly understand the reason behind information their partner offers if they take time to breathe and tune in to their body. The narrative is grounded in this sensory understanding of the truth. There should be silence and time between lines.

As clarity is achieved between the performers, the pace may pick up, but the focus should remain on building the dialogue one line at a time and not on blocking or space object work. CORE (character, objective, relationship, environment) need not be established right away but should be clear by the end of the scene, which can last from 3 to 7 minutes. If the performers seem to be struggling to establish these, they can be prompted for further clarity but you should wait as long as you can before doing this.

The Three-Person Version

This is another of my favorites. Try this after you have had success in the paired version. In this exercise, three chairs face the audience. Everything is the same except instead of looking at each other, the performers are facing outward and *cannot* look at each other. They need to tune in to their partners' content, tone of voice, and implied subtext. I usually assign a location where it makes sense that they wouldn't be looking at each other such as a wedding, jury box, or opera box for example. This version of the exercise is often hilarious as misunderstanding intention happens easily. As with the two-person version, slowing down and letting lines land is crucial. Once the first three *Sos* have been delivered, the performers can continue with one line at a time in no particular order. Remind them that they must respond to the last thing said. While it's natural they might be discussing a bride and groom, a trial, or an opera, we want to see how they feel about each other so they shouldn't let commentary about what they are seeing go on for longer than a couple of minutes.

Tips for So, So Scenes

- Explore what is said.
- Hear the intention behind the words.
- Pick up on everything.
- Let what your partner says land.
- Decide to feel something about what they just said every time. Nothing is neutral.
- Always respond to the last thing said.
- Not saying something can be a response.
- Cocreate. Find the story *with* your partner.
- Let the story develop line by line.
- Know that what your partner sees in you and states aloud is true. Say yes. Don't dismiss what they tell you.
- Don't self-protect or hide.

You can spend an entire rehearsal on the two versions of So, So Scenes. They are a palette cleanser and a clear example of how to be in second circle while doing narrative scenes. To build on this, let's explore the nuts and bolts that foster powerful improvised scenes.

Note

1. Calli McMurray, "Why the Brain Loves Stories," BrainFacts.org, www.brainfacts.org/neuroscience-in-society/the-arts-and-the-brain /2021/why-the-brain-loves-stories-030421.

6

OPENINGS, MIDDLES, AND ENDINGS

Three-Act Structure: A Macro View

In the opening scene of an improvised play, we meet characters who include the protagonist (the hero of the story we are following). The character who is emotionally or personally at risk during the first few moments of the opening scene is usually the protagonist.

To discover the protagonist, pay close attention to the actions and information provided by the performers in the opening scene and see what emerges. In a group scene, the physical position of the actors may identify the protagonist. Invariably someone will react strongly to something, or a particular piece of information will seem more important than another. Be watching and ready as this is where being present and in your body will be especially useful. Have your antenna fully extended for the slightest nuance to identify the lead.

If you are improvising a two-hour, three-act play, the timing can look something like this.

8:00 p.m. Scheduled start time.

8:05 p.m. Enter the stage and get the beginning suggestion from the audience. (We all try to start on time, but that never happens.)

8:10 p.m. Lights go down, the music swells, actors enter the stage, and your improvised story begins. Aim for a twenty-five-minute first act.

8:35 p.m. The second act needs to build in intensity. All the offers and characters introduced in the first act heighten until the climax of the second act, which takes us to intermission.

9:05–9:15 p.m. Intermission.

9:15–10:00 p.m. Third act. Bring it all home!

What will you do with your first act of approximately twenty-five minutes? You will most likely have 4–7 scenes in your first act. Following the thread in each current scene will help you know which scene should come next.

Entrances and Exits

Before you enter a scene in progress, check in with yourself. Is the story pulling you in or is it your brain telling you to go on? Breathe. Find second circle. No Kool-Aid. There must be a good rationale for entering, and the timing has to be right.

Why would you enter a scene that is in progress? Here are some reasons.

To catch someone in the act and raise the story's stakes.

Exercise: Working with your lighting and sound improviser, have an improviser start a scene in which they are doing something they shouldn't (opening a desk drawer, reading a letter, etc.). Have another improviser enter at just the right time to see what happens next. Discuss. You are trying to gain group insight about the timing of when to enter. What felt right? Is the group in agreement? Try it again.

To change the tone.

Exercise: Have one or two improvisers start a scene that has a very clear tone. Tone can mean somber, joyful, tense, raucous, and so on. Assign them a POV or emotion. Have a third improviser enter and change the tone with one line and their own personal energy. Practice breaking tension and lightening and darkening the mood. Discuss. Try it again.

To provide an obstacle for the lead or leads.

Exercise: Have one or two improvisers start a scene with a clear shared objective. Have another improviser enter and provide an obstacle that raises the stakes of the story rather than blocking the story itself. Discuss. Try it again.

To raise the stakes with a want, or to confess, or accuse.

Why leave a scene before the lights go down? Here are reasons.

- Your part is complete.
- Your exit provides an obstacle or may heighten the stakes.

- It's time to intentionally leave someone alone onstage to puzzle aloud or show their true nature.

Exercise: Do 1–2 minutes of the scene and then organically decide which character should leave the other alone. Once they are left alone, see what they do. This only works if they had clear POVs in the scene together before someone left. We may discover that the character's supposed POV was not what it seemed or it was hiding a deeper truth. Practicing talking aloud to yourself. It's a great skill for a longer narrative.

Varying Scenes

When standing offstage during a scene, you may have an idea as to what scene could come next. Hold it lightly. There still may be many clues in the scene currently underway that hint to what might come next. Stay in second circle, breathing and alert: something important might happen right before the lights go down and you will need to let go of your original idea and build on what just happened. The transitions will feel seamless if the ensemble members are attuned to each other and the tech improvisers.

When I'm watching a scene, there will be clues that tell me what type of scene should come next. It is a mix of energy shift and narrative needs.

You'll see genre-specific notes about tone later in this book, but generally speaking, you will want to vary the tone or energy of the scenes as you go along—sometimes between scenes or sometimes within a single scene. Has the tone been dark and now it needs to be balanced by something lighter? What kind of energy will provide a significant boost before intermission? You want to *feel* your way through the show rather than *think* your way through the show. You must be in a second circle state of mind to read the room and intuitively know what comes next.

Here are some examples of the sorts of tone shifts that can be effective.

Slow versus Fast

Example: We had a lovely slow scene in our rom-com so the next can be boisterous. Perhaps it's a buddy scene with high energy. Your story will tell you.

Exercise: Do a one-minute scene with a very clear pace and energy. Then have another improviser start a new scene with contrasting energy. The scenes should be part of one story but with varied pace and intensity. It's ideal if everyone is up on their feet and someone is working lights and sound.

Positive versus Negative

Example: We just had an ominous and tense scene in a noir and now we need a scene that provides some sweetness. What is pure or loving in this world and, therefore, at risk of destruction?

Exercise: Practice keeping the characters in the scene positive for as long as possible until an organic crack appears. Time the improvisers and make them stay positive as long as possible until we can't take it anymore. Discuss. Try it again.

Emotional Contrast

Example: The two lovers can't be together in our Chekhov play. They are staring at each other, and the tension is high. Having someone enter laughing at just the right time can alter the actors onstage and the tone of the story.

Exercise: Have an improviser enter a scene in progress. The performer should be aware of what emotional contrast they are bringing to the story, but make the character oblivious and unable to read the room.

Loud versus Quiet

Example: We had a fantastic car chase in a buddy action film. The music was loud, and the chase was thrilling. Now we can slow down and see how this action affected the buddies and their relationship. What has changed? Does one now respect the other more? Are they united in being in trouble with the chief?

Exercise: With accompanying lights and sound from your tech improvisers, practice a car chase or running scene then shift immediately into a second scene between the improvisers who were just in the action. Are they relieved? Are they at each other's throats? What narrative choices come out of our mouths after physical exertion?

Physical Positions and Staging

Example: During the last scene the actors sat down, so this time shake it up. Enter in a way and in a place that changes the visual and mental focus. Work in conjunction with your tech improviser on lights and sound.

Exercise: Have everyone up on their feet. Have the tech improviser darken the stage then bring up light on one part of the stage. Have some performers go to that spot to start a one-minute scene, followed by lights out, and then lights up on a different part of the stage where the performers should deliver a different scene. Do this several times. Use every bit of the stage, with or without furniture, up by the curtain, down on the lip of the stage, and do it lying down, sitting in a chair, standing in the middle, and so forth. Take note of how your physical placement creates story and character.

Transitions

The transitions between scenes can be one of the magical aspects of narrative improv. Work closely with your tech team in rehearsal as they provide transitions with lights and sound. Rehearse the following with your techs.

Split Focus on the Stage

For example, lit on one side of the stage, we see our rom-com lead confide to her best friend about the person she just met with 2–3 lines back and forth. The actors stay onstage as the lights go down and then up on a *different* part of the stage where we see the person she was talking about now talking to *their* best friend about her. Your tech will bring lights up and down on the scenes until it feels complete.

Flashbacks

Flashbacks are not in every genre, but if appropriate, an actor can initiate one. For example, "I remember the night of the accident so clearly." The actor starts to turn around as lights flash, and the music swells with other actors moving in slow motion as we return to the night of the accident.

Montage

Here's an example from the rom-com genre: After a one-line lead-in— "Let me show you New York"—upbeat music swells and the lights dip down then up as the actors start sightseeing. The music volume stays up. We don't want to hear the dialogue, but with lights dipping down and coming up, we keep changing locations as other actors come out and mime what they are doing, which implies place. Two chairs out and a waiter pouring wine signifies a restaurant. Other situations might include paddle boats, using binoculars, or buying hot dogs from a vendor, for example.

Offstage Sounds

Genre-appropriate music or sound effects that make narrative sense (traffic, sirens, crickets, ocean waves, street music, etc.) can be created by your tech improviser (or even by other performers on microphones) as the stage is in semi-darkness to keep the feeling of the place alive as we transition.

To Move or Not to Move? Chairs: A Personal Plea

Often improvisers move chairs on and off the stage between scenes, but I implore you not to do this in your long-form shows. It can destroy the transported feeling we just had when we see actors scurrying about a partly lit stage moving furniture. You can decide on playing areas in advance and stage furniture in those well-lit parts of the stage. In our workshop theater, I keep the middle open and then stage right has two chairs turned slightly toward each other, which can be a restaurant with an implied table in between, or two living room chairs, or something else. Stage left, I place a two-seater settee (not a couch) that can be a bed, car, and so forth. The actors can then leave the stage gracefully in blue transition light as they shift from their character to themselves standing on the side of the stage. If we blackout after a scene, we quickly transition to blue so the actors can enter and exit safely.

If you want to see the actors moving furniture, take note of Tony Kushner and Bertolt Brecht. As a playwright, Kushner prefers that theatricality be transparent. In his staging notes for *Angels in America*, he wrote,

> The plays benefit from a pared-down style of presentation, with scenery kept to an evocative and informative minimum. I recommend rapid scene shifts (no blackouts!) employing the cast as stagehands in shifting the scene. The moments of magic are to be fully imagined and realized as wonderful *theatrical* illusions—which means it's OK if the wires show. Maybe it's good that they do.

Kushner is an admirer of Brecht, who practiced a style of theatrical production whereby audiences were always reminded that they were in a theater. The choice to have no blackouts allows audiences to participate in the construction of a malleable theatrical world.

Middles: Messy or Mesmerizing?

At the end of your first act, you are twenty-five minutes in and can't stop to huddle and plan. You need to escalate the stakes and action to get us to intermission at your story's high (or low) point. If you have a solid first act, your middle should be easy. Usually it's not. Why is that?

Here's what I know after over thirty years in narrative improv. The struggle is real in the middle of a long-form narrative. Middles of *scenes* are even tricky sometimes, but why? It's imperative that you understand what needs to happen in the middle or second act of your story. Each genre will dictate the types of scenes that go in a second act. If it's a rom-com, there is usually a montage, and after that things get worse for our leads.

If you are in an improvised play, think of a pot on the stove. In the first act, the items in the pot are starting to boil, and maybe the stove top has a few splatters. The story is heating up. Now turn the dial up because in our second act, we want the lid to blow off the pot. Improvisers don't like the lid blowing off the pot because it's scary. If I let go, how will I bring this story home? You can't know. Your audience doesn't want to know . . . yet. And your characters definitely don't know how their story will end.

Why does the middle of an improvised story flatten? Sometimes, if improvisers get attached to the story unfolding in a certain way, they may tighten up and ignore where the *story* wants to go. This attempt to maintain the status quo until the third act creates a dullness onstage when the narrative stakes should be escalating. Understand and practice sustaining a physical connection to engage your audience and bring them on the ride. This requires a second circle mindset and leading with self 2 rather than self 1 (see chapter 2). The audience tends to remember the moments you created together rather than the whole narrative. Don't hang on to your ideas and miss the magic created by your ensemble improvising together effectively.

The middle feels different, and people find ways to resist it. You are too far in to go back and not close enough to the end to see the light. This is the point of no return. You have to go forward. This is where what is happening to the story's protagonist can mirror what the improvisers feel. You must let go of control. And you'll feel vulnerable, but in the middle of your improvised story, you must proceed confidently and embrace uncertainty rather than either tip-toe through or try to control the end too much. The middle is messy but it's also where all the magic happens.

Intermission

Once everyone has gathered in the dressing room, take a few moments for the energy to settle. Have a short (not judgmental) conversation about the show. Actors can repeat their character name and basic want but shouldn't discuss anything too specific—do not plan or coordinate in advance as this is a break of your implied contract with the audience and will drain the improvised narrative of its spontaneity and excitement. Pay attention to what insight your tech team has to offer. They have a better vantage point, watching you from the outside, and their opinions and ideas are invaluable.

Endings: Bring It All Home

In the genre sections in the last section of this book, you'll read about narrative elements that are specific to different genres. The genre dictates your story's tone and the ending. For example, rom-coms end happily with a monologue in the rain. In buddy action films, both buddies survive and have an increased appreciation for each other. Your noir story may end up with the protagonist killed, which will feel sad yet satisfying because we understand the stakes of that particular genre. If you killed off your leads in a rom-com, Jane Austen, or buddy action story, your audience would be perplexed and dissatisfied.

End a final scene, and therefore the story, with purpose. It should be evident by the third act whom we need to see and what needs to be faced and revealed to end this particular story satisfyingly. All the performers must be on the same page at this point. I can't tell you how many awkward endings I've seen when actors inserted so many new offers that the audience, or improvisers, couldn't possibly make sense of them in the five minutes that were left.

This is the crucial moment when every cast member, including the tech improvisers, needs to sync with a second circle mindset. Unfold your arms, don't lean against the wall on the side. Stand alert and ready in second, breathe, and you will know what needs to happen next.

For the final moment of a scene or a story, it's crucial to hold for a moment when you feel finished and exhale to allow time for the tech improviser to bring the lights down. Working together like this creates a magical feeling for everyone in the theater.

Post-Show Discussion

It's over! You ended the improvised play or film and are now ready for a post-show discussion.

If I'm directing or teaching a long-form show, I prefer to take notes during the show, greet the actors in the green room after the show, and then go home and go to bed and give notes later in rehearsal or via email. I like to provide notes *after* I've spent time reflecting on what I just saw. When this is impossible and I must give notes right after a show, I find it helpful to organize my notes in advance so my actors aren't watching me try to read what I scribbled in the dark. I divide a large piece of paper into three columns. The left-hand column is headed "What Worked"; the middle column is headed "What Almost Worked"; and the far-right column is headed "What Didn't Work." While watching the show, I place my quick thoughts in the applicable column. When vulnerable faces, flushed with excitement, are looking to me for leadership and guidance, I can start with everything that worked. There are always moments to celebrate. Using the What Almost Worked column, I can guide and illuminate other roads not taken. For the What Didn't Work column, as I'm giving notes, sometimes I might say, "I wrote this note down, but then because of that, this led to this other thing that worked so . . ." Notes are, of course, subjective. I believe in being honest and encouraging. Mistakes are opportunities to learn or laugh. In narrative improv, we are in a gray area, not black and white. I firmly believe in clarifying what the improviser is doing well then giving them the next instruction that builds from there.

Years ago I was directing a student group in the fish-out-of-water genre. In the final scene, some villagers finished their catapult and won a competing village's catapult competition. Someone offered the idea for everyone to get in the catapult and fling themselves to the other town. This sounds crazy now, but it made perfect sense as a way to end the story with energy and fun. I sat in the audience and watched the improvisers negotiate for several minutes getting in and out of the catapult and discussing why and why not to do it. The lighting improviser was poised to bring the lights down if they did indeed get into the catapult—ideally there would be a countdown and then, in slow motion, the performers would rise up in the air, the lights would go down, and the music would swell. The end. Or so it should have been. Instead they talked for a long time and then walked off the stage, never getting in the catapult. I sat there in shock. It was truly a terrible ending for an enjoyable, energized show. I entered the green room, they looked up at me, and we all burst out laughing. It was so bad. They knew it was bad. They each had reasons for not getting into the catapult, but I remember that they weren't certain how to make it look like they were flying in the air. They didn't trust their lighting and sound improviser to have their back. We laughed so hard together. They learned the lesson and I still remember that show years later.

It is crucial that performers keep in mind the guidelines below for how to process show notes or talk to each other post show.

- Focus on *your* work first and recognize if you were in first, second, or third circle.
- Own your insecurity and judgment.

- If other performers are celebrating and you think it was a rough show, just take everything in. It's okay to be quiet now, go home, eat, and go to bed. You will have more perspective in the morning.

- If the show sticks with you the next day, keep unpacking that. Do you feel hurt? Using all the tools from this book thus far, talk privately with your teacher or director if you are having trouble understanding your response to a show. You were having a group experience and an individual experience at the same time. Do not gossip or judge others in this vulnerable stage; learn the lesson you need for next time, and then let go.

- Do not recruit others to create a gossip train. That is ensemble poison.

Working with Technical Improvisers

"People will say to keep it simple and just hit the beats. Fuck 'em. Have fun, take some risks, and make some mistakes. You're as much a part of the show as the people on the stage."
—**Jason Murphy**

It is impossible to improvise a full-length story without support from the tech booth. When I first started the Improvising Plays & Films Lab in 2003, I quickly realized that we needed to score our scenes with music and bring the lights up and down to create a theatrical atmosphere. I was fortunate to have three students who volunteered to help with this task. Jim Babcock helped hang lights with dimmers, and Glenn Camhi and Jason Murphy used their incredible musical knowledge to find the perfect music for whatever genre we were exploring. The effect was immediate. With sound creating tone and lights assisting the theatricality of the moment, it allowed the improvisers to speak less and connect with their bodies more. The result was palpable.

Your rehearsal period must include your tech improvisers. Once your show begins, they direct the show. They follow the action and can push the actors to emotional places with their music and light choices. Help your tech team understand the genre and your directorial intention. Everyone in the ensemble should spend time in the tech booth as it gives the improvisers a better understanding of what the tech crew needs from them while onstage. A tech improviser may wait for an actor to stop talking, exhale, turn and look out, or leave before they bring the lights down. Work with your tech improvisers in rehearsal and develop a shared language.

Here's some of what Impro Theatre's incredible former tech team had to say:

> *"As technical improvisers, we have a unique perspective to observe the show from the outside and are simultaneously on stage in spirit. Our calls support the ensemble and can energize the stage. When we are completely in second circle, it feels like magic."*—**Arlo Sanders**

"Commit to your choices in the booth as fiercely as you would onstage! Even if it's the wrong tone or look for the moment, the improvisers onstage can better use a bold choice than a timid one. If you are patient and brave, those miscues will often lead to something no one could have planned for—and that's where the magic happens. I'd much rather hear the wrong cue at the right time than the perfect cue several beats too late.

Directors undoubtedly will have a vision, but I'd encourage all of them to let their tech improvisers play and experiment the same way they would the rest of the ensemble. For whatever reason, tech receives less berth to make mistakes. Instead of micromanaging their choices before they've had a chance to make them, let them feel it out. Knowing that the director and ensemble trust you enough to play is the only way to exist as a tech improviser. Otherwise, you're just an operator doing as instructed."—**Alex Caan**

"Be upfront with your tech at the beginning of the process. The more clarity and communication, the better the show will be. Do you already have a preset music list and lighting idea? Or do you want your tech to explore the music themselves and bring their ideas to the table? Communicate expectations and creative ideas with your tech and allow them space to add their touch just as you would if they were an improviser onstage."—**Emily Jacobsen**

"I would spend hours at the boards when no one was in the theater and when the stage was being set for its upcoming weekend of shows. With most avenues, it comes down to knowledge and practice. You learn the equipment to burn it down gloriously and triumphantly. On top of lighting, a great tech is a colorist, composer, and chronologist . . . the unseen actor and editor rolled into one. Once the audience forgets you are there, you hit the sweet spot. We live on the edge of our seats in the booth because when you position yourself on the precipice, you must be ready to jump off with the actors at any moment."—**Cory Wyszynski**

PART II

THE TANGIBLE *MUST HAVES* TO BE SUCCESSFUL AT GOING LONG

7

EXERCISES TO FIND AND DEVELOP SECOND CIRCLE

One of the biggest challenges in narrative improv is not to get lost in your head as you stand on the side of the stage. I constantly adjust my posture, arms, and breath as I observe the scene in progress. Ideally, instead of leaning against the wall with arms folded mulling over potential choices, you are standing alert, listening, and breathing with your arms open. Consider this state as an energized second circle. If we start thinking or planning, we will miss the current moment, and our bodies will reflect that. Invite self 1 to join you *in* your body (self 2). If you're in an audience, you can tell the present state of the improvisers from their stance on the side of the stage. It's essential that a performer trust that they will intuitively know when to enter the scene or when to stay off when they are in second circle. Trust is integral to what we do; nothing will throw you when you surf the moment in second circle.

In the first section of this book, I went into great detail on the mental and physical state needed to find and maintain second circle, which is essential to creating an improvised play at the highest level. This chapter contains the exercises that will enable you to do this.

When trying to find your presence, it's important to start with the body first. Connecting to your body is essential for being in the here and now. The body can only be in the present; it doesn't know how to be in the past or future. Your mind pulls you into the past, obsessing over what's gone before or worrying about the future. Your body is what connects you to the current moment. When you find yourself in your head, bring yourself back to the body through posture and breath adjustments. The following physical exercises are tools for staying connected to the present moment. Finding second circle goes like this: body first because the body houses the breath, then breath because the breath activates the voice.

Exercises for the Body

The Second Circle Stance

- feet: Plant both feet on the floor, almost parallel, and under your hips. Your toes should be pointed forward. Direct your energy—not your weight—forward on the balls of the feet but with your heels still on the floor. Rock back and forth between the balls of the feet and the heels until you can feel the middle.
- knees: unlocked (i.e., lock your knees and release them 7 percent)
- hips: tucked under, not thrust forward
- spine: up, neither slumped nor rigidly held
- shoulders: released, not rounded

- arms: loosely hanging at your side. Your fingertips should be touching the sides of your thighs.
- head: balanced with ease, on top of the spine; soft gaze directly ahead; chin parallel to the ground
- jaw: unclenched, with the lips lightly touching

Stand in second circle for a few moments and breathe, getting used to the silence and becoming comfortable in the pose. As you stand in second, ask yourself,

- "How do I feel?" People often say "balanced," "grounded," "calm," "ready"—things like that. If this is not your habitual pose it may feel odd. If so, take more time to breathe in second.
- "How does the room feel?" You might feel more connected to the space you are in.
- "How does my connection to the group feel?" If you are with others, note how you feel with them so you can contrast that to first and third.

Now that you've *felt* second, stand in first.

The First Circle Stance

- feet: very narrow stance. Your feet are touching. Your energy should be focused back on your heels.
- spine: slumped
- shoulders: rounded forward and slumped
- arms: folded or in a defensive position
- head: looking down to avoid eye contact
- jaw: clenched

Stand in first for a few moments and breathe, feeling your body, the presence of others if you are not alone, and the room itself. As you stand in first, ask yourself,

- "How do I feel?" People often say "uncertain," "closed," "doubtful," or "shy," for example. If this is your habitual pose it may feel good. Sometimes people say they feel better in first. Note that you always have first to come back to if you need to reenergize yourself (for us introverts) or to feel protected. First is not ideal for communicating with or connecting to others. This is important to know. You have a choice on how you show up and whether you invite connection or not.
- "How does the room feel?"
- "How does my connection to the group feel?"

Now that you've *felt* first, stand in third.

Third Circle Stance

- feet: in a wide stance, wider than your hips. Take as much space as you can.
- energy: focused forward on the balls of your feet
- spine: rigidly held up
- chest: puffed up and pushed out
- arms: up and ready to engage
- head: up and aggressively making eye contact. Aim not to be the first one to break eye contact with anyone else.
- jaw: clenched

As you stand in third, ask yourself,

- "How do I feel?" People often say "strong," "aggressive," "pushy," "tight." If this is your habitual pose it may feel good because it is familiar, but know that third can push others away or unhelpfully take control of the room. Third doesn't invite collaboration. A third circle person once said to me, "I don't collaborate, I dominate." Noted.
- "How does the room feel?"
- "How does my connection to the group feel?"

Now that you've *felt* third, shake it off, stand back in second, and take a breath.

Now find first, second, and third energy through movement. Doing the following saloon doors exercise is an excellent way to start.

Moving Using Swinging Saloon Doors

Saloon doors—chest-high doors that swing in both directions—provide the basis for a useful second circle exercise because the doors give feedback. *How* you enter determines how the doors respond. In the following exercise, imagine there is a pair of saloon doors in front of you.

- Shift your body into first circle. On the count of three, move through the saloon doors as someone in first would and then stop. (Sometimes folks don't fully make it on the other side of the doors because of their first circle behavior.) Take a moment and look around. How do you feel? How does the room feel? (Words commonly used are *uncertain, afraid, timid, alone,* and *careful.*)

- Go back to where you were standing and shift your body into third. On the count of three, enter through the saloon doors in third. (There are often a few kicks to the doors or mock gunfire from performers doing this exercise.) Take a moment, and have a look around. Describe how you feel or how the room feels from this perspective. (I usually hear words or phrases like *aggressive; looking for a fight; powerful; strong; in charge;* and *impatient.*)

- Return and shift your body into second. On the count of three, enter through the saloon doors in second. Take a moment, and have a look around. Describe how you feel or how the room feels from this state of presence. (Words that tend to come up here are *connected, equal, ready, present,* and *energized.*)

- Take a moment to reflect on this exercise. Sometimes there is a shift in perception regarding third circle's power versus second's power. Some might say they feel more potent in third than in second. Discuss what power means and the type of strength required in a second circle improviser. Do you want to overpower your partners or play *with* them? Typically people feel a part of the whole in second; they feel seen and relaxed; the room feels safe; and so on. The goal is to feel the differences between first, second, and third in your body, in space, and in relation to each other.

Let's layer in more movement to find second.

Walking Onstage in Second Circle

Before you start walking in second, take a breath and soften your gaze, allowing your vision to widen, taking in everything at once rather than focusing on anything in particular. This way of seeing is called *lantern focus*. Imagine a lantern on the stage. Turn it on, and it would spill light out in all directions. The opposite of this is *spotlight focus*, which means you focus your eyes and attention on one thing. When doing this exercise, you want to use lantern focus and not spotlight focus to see the space as a whole and the other actors within the area. In lantern focus, the aim is to see and feel everything in the room without effort.

- Have your group gather on one side of the stage, standing and breathing in second.
- Have one performer start walking on the stage, remaining in second circle.
- Then one by one, as it *feels* right to each performer, each person adds themselves to the group onstage, with everyone still walking in second.
- Keep your heads up, chins parallel with the floor, not making eye contact but holding lantern focus, taking in everything and nothing in particular.
- Once everyone onstage is walking, have someone offstage read a script similar to the following.

Walk in second, with energy and purpose as though you have somewhere to go. Breathe easily. Keep walking around the space, and when you feel energized in your body, come to a standstill, but don't try to brace or lock your body. You are still, but not stopped, in a state of readiness. You feel alive and alert with energy through your back. The whole space around you is available. You know and feel what's going on around you, seeing the space clearly in this state.

- Next, the group should focus on starts, stops, and walking through doorways. Read a script similar to this one.

Your doorway is only open if you can pass through it without contacting anyone or adjusting your body. You may intend to walk forward, but then someone crosses your path. If you would have to adjust your body to move around that person, then your doorway is closed, and you should stop. Let go of where you intended to go and respond to the situation as it is rather than how you wish it were. Remain in place until your gut tells you to move again.

When the performers resume movement, it should not be a mental decision—for example, "I think I should move"—but a physical response to the stimuli around them. Having them do this, the ensemble's energy is connected, which helps them *feel* their way rather than think their way through each moment onstage.

I suggest warming up this way before a rehearsal or show. When the show starts, maintain lantern focus but dim it down so you can layer spotlight focus on your scene partners. Lantern focus will keep your energy in the space as a whole, enabling your felt presence. Spotlight focus will ensure you are engaged viscerally with your scene partners. During rehearsals, practice lantern and spotlight focus one at a time until you are naturally able to deploy both.

Exercises for the Breath

"I worked with an acting coach named Harold Guskin, who started by talking to me about breathing and how we

use the breath to control our feelings. He walked me through an exercise mimicking what we tend to do emotionally when we start to feel emotional—basically, to hold our breath. The goal of the exercise was to help me understand how to take whatever emotion was in the scene and connect it with my physical being. As I was sitting there with him, I became aware of how much I held my breath. A quick breath out, then in, and hold it: I'd been doing that for years whenever I was pricked by fear or sorrow or rage. I'd shut down my emotions by using my breath to literally keep my feelings inside."—**Demi Moore**

One night I was at Max's Opera Café in San Francisco. The waiters and waitresses there are also opera singers, so occasionally they break out into song. I was with my mom and fiancé when I heard someone start to sing "Happy Birthday" behind me. Because my birthday was close and the person was singing in my ear, I assumed they had planned this for me. I looked at them shaking my head as if to say, "You guys . . ." then turned around only to see the back of the waitress singing to the table behind us. Her voice resonated in her body so completely that it sounded like she was singing in my ear. The realization—"Oh, this is what my body is capable of if I allow it"—is still with me many years later.

What good is a second circle body if no one can hear you when you speak? For some reason, a proper second circle breath has been a real challenge for me. I tend to hold my breath when I am driving and daydreaming, suddenly finding myself breathing shallowly, and this carried over into my acting. In 2006 I was diagnosed with adult onset intermittent asthma. My doctor practiced Western medicine, and yet he first said to me, "Grief is held in the lungs. Has anything been going on for you this year?" I said no and then burst into tears. I am grateful to my doctor for helping me treat the symptoms and inviting me to look deeper at what might be causing the problem. I invite you to do the same. Get curious about the mind-body connection. Yes, you can agree to take deeper breaths and learn how to breathe better, but the *why* behind what holds us back is worth your investigation. Meditation and breathwork can offer invaluable breakthroughs for the person aware of under-breathing.

You will notice who is holding their breath when you run exercises or rehearse in second circle. We unconsciously mimic the breathing patterns of those around us, and if you find yourself out of breath, it may indicate that you have breath-holders in your midst. A good check-in is for whoever is leading the exercise or rehearsal to ask if everyone is breathing. This will probably get a few laughs, which automatically deepens the breath. Breathing deeply helps quiet the thinking mind. There is nothing to figure out; just mindfully breathe in and out. A yawn can be an indication that the mind is over engaged. Having members of the group let out an audible sigh or laugh loudly together can help to disconnect the mind. You want to release physical tension from the body. The thinking brain can conjure many reasons why deep breathing is terrible—it will make you dizzy or emotional and so on. Emotions ride on the breath. If you start to feel emotions while doing these exercises, using second circle breath will allow you to accept what is happening rather than resist it.

There is a great need for you to know how to harness the power of the exhale. The breath powers the voice!

Try this exercise.

Increase the Length of Your Exhale

This technique from *Breath* by James Nestor helps engage more movement from the diaphragm and increases respiratory efficiency. It should never be forced. Each breath should feel soft and enriching.

- Sit up so your chin is straight and perpendicular to your spine.
- Take a gentle breath through your nose.
- At the top of the breath, begin counting softly aloud from 1 to 10 and each time you reach 10 begin counting again at 1.
- As you reach the natural conclusion of the exhale, keep counting but do so in a whisper, letting your voice softly trail away. Then keep going until only your lips are moving and your lungs feel completely empty.
- Take in another large, soft breath and begin counting again.
- Continue for 30 cycles. (If that's too many, begin with 10 cycles and each day add another until you get up to 30.)
- Once you feel comfortable doing this in a sitting position, try it while walking, jogging, or doing other light exercises.

Wall Pose

In this exercise, everyone holds a particular pose and focuses on their breathing. When I lead the exercise, I usually have group members stay there for about a minute. When we are done and come back together, many have naturally transitioned into second. I don't debrief much here; I want them to stay in their bodies and not activate their thinking brains.

- Have everyone in your group go to a wall and stand an arm's length away with their palms flat on the wall.

- Each person should slowly flex their triceps, bringing their face closer to the wall. It's like you are doing yoga plank, but on the wall, not the ground. Then you bend your arms and hold as you breathe deeply.

- Each person holds the pose there, about three inches from the wall, and breathes. Usually the first breath is a deep belly breath; ideally you continue breathing with this deep breath throughout the exercise. If there is resistance and the breath is not going to the belly, place it there with intention and try to maintain that belly breath.

Breathe to the Hand, the Wall, and the Space

Have everyone stand in a circle and shift their body into a second circle posture before doing the following exercise, which lasts about five minutes.

- Relax your jaw and let your mouth drop open.
- Put your palm in front of your mouth. Look at your hand and concentrate on sending your breath to it. You will feel the moment the breath connects to your hand, relaxing your cerebral cortex and transmitting a feeling of well-being throughout your body.
- Now shift your body into first circle. Allow your breath to become shallow. Your breath should not be touching the palm of your hand; it should stop halfway. Listen for a few moments

to feel how this shallow breathing affects your whole body and the room. Then shake it off.

- Now shift your body into third circle. Allow your breath to get loud and forceful. Often people will cough or be unable to sustain this; try to listen to feel how over-breathing affects your body and the room. Shake it off.

- Now shift your body back into second circle. Your breath lightly touches your palm again.

- Little by little, begin moving your hand farther away, continuing to send your breath to the palm of your hand. Once your arm is outstretched, let it drop to your side but continue breathing until your breath reaches one of the walls of the room that is in your line of vision. Now with each subsequent breath, imagine you can breathe onto a larger and larger area on the wall until you are breathing to the entire wall. Expand the site you breathe onto until it encompasses the ceiling, the floor, and even the area behind you. This expansive breathing is what is meant by breathing in second.

All great performers and speakers breathe the whole space; they don't breathe half the room or beyond the room as this would disconnect them. If you remember to breathe into the entire room you are working in and any new places you enter, your presence will be palpable. For example, if you breathe the space as you enter a room for an audition, show, or presentation, you will make a stronger impression. As you shake hands with someone, focus on breathing to them in the same way, and they will register you sooner and remember your name better. You will notice that you can draw a first or third circle person's energy into second if you breathe to them.

Breath Bath

This exercise is about the connection that rides on the breath and how we can make each other feel supported or abandoned. When improvising a play, we often stand on the side, watching the improvisers onstage. We have to be in an energized second, listening and seeing everything. Those onstage *feel* when we go into first circle thinking—over-evaluating—or into third circle, which can cause frustration. The call to stay in second circle is vital to the show's success.

- Stand in a circle shoulder to shoulder.
- Ask for a volunteer to go into the center.
- Close the gap in the circle.
- Ask the volunteer to stand in the center with closed eyes (this is optional) and breathe in second.
- Have everyone on the perimeter stand and breathe in second to the person in the center.
- After about a minute of breathing, the person in the middle should slowly open their eyes (if they're closed) and switch places with another volunteer. Do this with three volunteers, each one ending their time in the middle when it feels right.
- When finished, expand the circle so the group is not touching arms.
- Ask the three volunteers what they noticed and how it felt to be in the center. Here are some of the comments I've heard.
  - "I felt warm."
  - "I felt supported."
  - "There were cold pockets and warm pockets."

- "I felt connected to everyone."
- "I noticed how busy my brain was and had to keep returning to my breath."

More Breathing Exercises

Do one or all these breathing exercises sitting comfortably or standing.

Falling Out Breath

Excellent for releasing physical tension in the body.

- Take a deep breath in, filling your lungs as much as possible.
- At the top of your breath, take one more sip of air.
- Exhale with a big, out-loud sigh (something like *HHHAAAA*) as you release all the air. You are sighing out loud on the exhale.

Box Breath

This one helps increase mindfulness.

- Inhale to the count of four.
- Hold your breath at the top of the count of four.
- Exhale to the count of four.
- Hold your breath at the bottom of the count to four.
- Repeat at least three times—or more if you want.

Emptying the Breath

This *activates* the parasympathetic nervous system and *calms* your sympathetic nervous system.

- Inhale to the count of three.
- Exhale slowly to the count of six, releasing as much air as possible.
- Repeat as many times as feels right for you.

Placing the Voice in Second Circle

"'Mean what you say' is a phrase you said to me that I would never forget. It sounds simple at first, but it resonated with me in a more significant way. It influenced my performances from then on. From being a performer who was told they thrive on jokes, sometimes to the detriment of other performers, it took me to the next level. To expand on the phrase, I was able to take what I felt I was good at and ground it more to the benefit of the audience and the improvising team. I haven't forgotten that seemingly mundane phrase, and I've evolved it in my further studies. Thank you for saying it to me!"
—Torrey Halverson

When the breath is in second circle, you can use it to activate your voice. The power of the voice starts in the breath, and the deeper the breath, the stronger the voice. So scientifically the voice is powered from the stomach but the sound starts in the throat.

When the voice is in second circle, you will impact your scene partner and the audience. As improvisers, we know that nerves are a part of being vulnerable onstage without a script. These nerves can overpower us and get in the way of our effectiveness. However, if you prepare the body, breath, and voice for the nerves' arrival, you won't get Elvis-leg, shaky hands, or a wobbly voice. The discipline of relaxing the body, breath, and voice will help you assimilate adrenaline rushes and use them to facilitate charisma while onstage. The goal is to be open to inspiration at all times, and to achieve this, you need to prepare yourself to receive it.

One of the quickest ways to move your voice into second involves using the cork from a bottle of wine or olive oil. Many years ago I booked a voiceover job and my call time was early in the morning. I warmed my voice up in the car, but it still wasn't where it needed to be. I had noticed on other voice jobs that how my voice sounded in the middle of the session was where I needed to start. Very often they would have me go back to the beginning and re-record early lines with my fuller sound.

What does having a full voice mean? I've been coaching people on their voices for over thirty years. When I hear someone speak, I can't help but see a circle. Their voice is either filling out the circle or it's missing a section. Usually the lower one-third of the circle that I envision is absent, or their full sound is not there. Think of the megaphone a cheerleader uses. That's how we should use our mouths to transfer a sound that leaves us and reaches our listeners. Some of us, because we learn speaking through imitation, do not speak in a way that serves us. Do this cork exercise, and I promise the sound that comes out of you when you take the cork out will be your voice in second. Your volume will increase and your voice will sound clear. Try it!

Cork It! Individual Version

A structural stretch exercise to reduce excess jaw tension and relax the throat.

- Place the cork between your front teeth—not too far back, to allow room for your tongue to move.
- Begin talking with the cork in your mouth.
- Remove the cork after thirty seconds and continue talking. After ten seconds, place the cork back in and so forth for a few minutes. I usually set a timer. I need about five minutes minimum to hear a shift in my voice. The longer I do it, the longer the voice change lasts.
- Often, as the exercise progresses, you will feel and hear your voice move forward from the back of the mouth. Your volume will increase. You'll feel more comfortable to be louder. Your words will sound crisp and your voice will become resonant and full, all in a brief amount of time. You are using your mouth as a megaphone, which is how it is intended.

Cork It! Group Version

- After the individual version has been demonstrated, performers pair up and spread around the room.
- Each participant is given a cork that they will keep.
- Have them decide who will go first in their pair.
- This person will start with the cork in their mouth.
- The partner without the cork will listen to how their speaking partner's voice changes every time they take the cork out and speak. Do this for about three minutes.

- When the first person finishes, give their partner a minute to share feedback on the vocal changes they heard.
- Once both partners have spoken with a cork, the performers stand in a circle and are invited to describe their experience. How did their voice sound and feel by the end of the exercise? How did their partner's voice sound change during the activity?

When I lead this exercise I usually feel my way through it, but I often have everyone keep the cork in for thirty seconds, out for ten seconds, and then repeat until the time is up. I do this every class until they have it down, and then I ask them to "cork" on the way to class so they arrive with their voices in second circle.

Heart versus Head Language

"My native language is Arabic, and even though I am fluent in English, improvising in English always felt a little removed. I was successful in it, but it never felt 100 percent authentic to me. In one of our classes, Jo suggested I try to do a monologue in Arabic (with a prompt of Being Desperate). As soon as I started talking in my native tongue, I completely transformed. It felt much more real. I was invoking my hands in a way I never did while improvising in English, using idioms that connected me with my roots. It was a liberating and exhilarating experience at the same time. I have tried to carry that feeling with me when I improvise (in either language) and help me become a more authentic actor and improviser."
—Basel Al-Naffouri

Not long ago I was teaching an entry-level improv class with a wide variety of nationalities and with half the class speaking English as their second language. As they began doing scenes together, it quickly became evident that we had a challenge. Two students, in particular, were speaking from their heads and not their hearts, and their scenes were falling flat. I suggested they do a scene together each speaking in their native language (Korean and Spanish) and see where that took them. Neither of them spoke the other's language. It remains one of the most emotional and funny scenes I've ever seen. They ended up as a couple trying to rearrange the furniture in their living room. Because they couldn't understand each other's words, they also had to use body language to get their points across. The mundane task of rearranging furniture became something we all related to, and their performance was utterly believable. I wanted them to feel what it was like to improvise in their heart language to bring that feeling to their performances in English. Their improv level greatly improved.

I was also coaching an improviser in passion noir, and he was trying to find his *homme fatale*—his leading man status. When he spoke, it just didn't land on his partner or the room. I asked him to monologue in his first language (Arabic), and by the end, there wasn't a dry eye in the house. The heart connection was immediate. He could now feel the difference between head and heart and adjust accordingly when his scenes weren't working. For those with only one language, our reset may simply be to take a breath and feel and mean the next words out of our mouth.

Since your ensemble is delving into narrative improv, we must believe you when you speak. Who wants to watch an entire improvised play where nothing sounds true? We want to believe what you say onstage. Be brave, feel the truth, and say it aloud for all to hear.

8

CREATE THE TEAM THAT CAN
DO THIS WORK TOGETHER

The Neuroscience of Trust

One of the many benefits of second circle is that it cultivates feelings and behavior that engender trust. Trust is an essential element of improv, and studying neurological signals helps us understand when and how trust works. The following eight steps come from Paul J. Zaks's article in the *Harvard Business Review*, "The Neuroscience of Trust."

Eight Steps to Build Trust

1. Recognize excellence.
2. Induce challenge stress.
3. Allow people discretion in how they do their work.
4. Enable job crafting.
5. Share information broadly.
6. Intentionally build relationships.
7. Facilitate whole-person growth.
8. Show vulnerability.

Recognize Excellence

When working with an established ensemble, the following exercise recognizes each individual's strengths as seen by their peers.

- Sit in a circle.
- Ask someone to take notes (to be given to participants later).
- Ask for a volunteer to go first. Let's assume our volunteer is Ahsan.
- Ask the group, "What does Ahsan naturally bring to the ensemble and the stage?"
- Allow time for everyone who wants to speak. They might say, "Ahsan brings bravery, fun, and energy." "He's always on time, and thoughtful." "His characters are grounded and real." The notetaker should write these down to give to Ahsan later.
- Then ask, "What can Ahsan add to what he already brings?" They might say, "He could add dangerous characters or more edge to the stage." "He could express more extreme emotions."

This process is an excellent opportunity for Ahsan to hear what he does well, as well as receive encouragement in areas he might explore. I have found that once a performer knows what the group loves about them, they take on new challenges with increased confidence. They may be asked to add different types of characters or other qualities of being, and they are usually eager to work.

I've never had anyone say anything harmful or inappropriate during this exercise, but you are there to make sure it's a safe space for everyone. Go through each person in the group. For a twelve-person group, this takes about 75–90 minutes, but the rewards are plentiful. Clearly stating behaviors that are positive and offering specific areas for growth is key to keeping your team of improvisers inspired and connected.

Induce Challenge Stress

What we do in improv encourages working together, surmounting challenges, and reaching a specific goal or endpoint. The challenge of achieving a clear goal together naturally enhances group cohesion and effective collaboration. Take the time with your team to celebrate when you've just accomplished something together. Whether a longer story or a selection of scenes, acknowledging success releases neurochemicals that strengthen focus and the improvisers' connection with each other. Don't rush on to the next challenge without celebrating the good that just happened.

Allow People Discretion in How They Do Their Work

When a group is working on a particular genre, it's ideal to delegate research or ask performers to create exercises and teach them to the group. Encourage performers to contribute ideas for how to bring something alive onstage or to decide which genre tropes might be problematic in the current climate.

Enable Job Crafting

As your ensemble grows together in strength and knowledge, performers should be asked what genres they would like to explore or invited to take turns leading the group in their favorite warm-ups. I have often mentored up-and-coming improv groups in the genre or story style of their choice, which allows me to not only share my years of genre exploration but discover genres that are new to me. "Game of Thrones" and "The Next Generation" are now two of my favorites (thank you, Sara, Paul, Matt, Aliza, and Madi!).

Share Information Broadly

If you have an improv school, have curriculum progression stated clearly on your website. Check in regularly with students about their goals and agree on how to go forward together. One good way to do this is to side coach during scenes instead of after. I recommend having clear class time in which you let students know you will side coach in real time and then having a time in class when you don't give notes at all but just allow them to improvise and see if they are self directing. As show dates approach, I side coach less and less so they get used to handling whatever shows up on their own.

When I'm side coaching during a scene, I side coach in real time as much as possible. This way, performers can redirect on their feet and experience the adjustment. While you are watching a scene and have a note to give, wait a moment to see if they do it themselves. If not, you can say, "Soft freeze—Eric, come downstage into the light and say that"; or "Soft freeze—everyone be silent for a moment and take Mieko's offer in before you respond"; or "Derek, enter again and take in what Basel is doing in the room as you enter—let that affect you immediately." The directions should be quick and clear so performers can adjust immediately and experience your suggestion and the effect it has on the scene. This is all subjective—you won't always be right. Don't try to be right, just offer what you have at the moment.

When giving notes after a scene, keep the following in mind.

- Your notes are ideally based on process rather than content. The scene will never happen again so it's a bit useless to focus on micro content. It drives me crazy after a scene to hear a director or teacher say, "What I would have liked to see . . ." If you need to direct the students to hit certain narrative beats for a specific genre, do it in the moment. Do not torture everyone with all the great things they could have done if they had been in your head while they were performing. Embrace what showed up rather than lament missed opportunities.

- Give specific notes to individuals and help them with their improv mindset. Remind them of what worked and build from there. Point out other choices that were available that they didn't see or take.

- Tell the ensemble about their group patterns and help break those, as well, where necessary. Do the same people start every show? First and third circle patterns are important to point out. Teach all of them how to start and stay in second.

- Note the mistakes that turned into gifts.

- Remind them to hold it lightly and let go of getting it right. After all, improv is disposable theater.

Intentionally Build Relationships

Life-long friendships and relationships often come out of improv, and this is truly life changing. If the ensemble turns negative or their post-rehearsal drinks turn into giving each other notes or gossip, this can create a toxic culture. Another invaluable skill is to turn complaints into requests. Try to move beyond complaining and be able to express what you want instead. As you listen to complaints from others, try to tease out what it is they want rather than what they do not want. These skills will go a long way to ensure your ensemble's longevity. Strive to know each other on a deeper level.

At one point I was teaching a very diverse class. I had one student who was older and spoke very little English. He could only say yes and smile, which made it challenging to move scenes forward. He was a cheerful man, but I noticed the students were slow to join him for scenes. Typically, in the last thirty minutes of class, I would have students interview each other with the pronoun switching exercise (see below). During the interview, he revealed that he had escaped from North Korea under gunfire, had almost starved at sea, and had barely made it to New York, where he worked three jobs while going to medical school. His story was riveting, and following this revelation, students eagerly jumped up to do scenes with him. He still had the same limitations with language, but the students now worked with him successfully because they were able to see him fully rather than through a limited lens. Seeing the humanity in each other, feeling empathy, putting ourselves in other people's shoes—this is second circle.

The following exercises build relationships within the group.

Interviews with Pronoun Switching

I've explored dozens of listening exercises over the past thirty years looking for experiential training around second circle listening. The following is my absolute favorite in this category. I created it by accidentally misinterpreting another exercise. Mistakes really are gifts! The pronoun shift creates a visceral feeling of second circle listening and empathy toward another ensemble member. One person gives their story away and another person takes that story on.

- Everyone in the room pairs off and sits in chairs across from each other with their knees reasonably close together. The room will get loud so the pairs should be as far away from each other as possible.
- Each pair decides who is going first, and that person raises their hand so it's clear who is starting.
- The person starting is the interviewer. They are going to interview their partner and take on their story as they do it. To do this, they will change pronouns. As they interview their partner, they will say the pronoun *I* instead of *you*. For example, they might say, "What was I like in second grade?" The person answering uses the pronoun *you* instead of *I* even though they are talking about themselves. "You loved reading and reorganizing your bedroom on Saturdays."
- The interview goes on for about five minutes, and then the interviewer and interviewee switch roles.

Here are some things to watch for:

- I recommend asking questions about ages 1 month old to 20 years old and staying away from work.
- Try not to jump around. It's a short exercise, and there is no way to get a whole life story. Just start somewhere and build from there.
- The interviewer can't know what their next question will be until they hear their partner's answer. If they are in second circle, they will know what to ask next.

- Remember that you are not improvising yet! The interviewee is telling the truth about their lives, and both pair members are experiencing second circle connection and listening.

I usually take 5 minutes to explain the exercise, 10 minutes to do it (5 minutes per person), and 10 minutes for a group debrief. The debriefs from these are fantastic. *Empathy* is a word that always comes up—empathy for your partner and yourself. Excellent debrief questions include What was it like to take on someone else's story? and What was it like to give your story away?

People might mention feeling compassion for themselves or not being self-conscious about themselves (thus avoiding first circle) because they were just giving their partner information they needed. They might also realize how much they have in common. Some folks find it hard not to interrupt and share their similar story (third circle) so it's an excellent opportunity for them to experience pure listening.

Topic Talk

Topic talk is a great way to get the ensemble to know each other better. You can do this in various ways.

- Print the sheet of topic questions below. Sit in a circle and ask someone for a number between 1 and 47 and then read the corresponding question aloud. Give them one minute to answer.
- Or have everyone in pairs around the room. One person tells their partners their answers and then they switch.
- Once an ensemble knows each other well, do this paired with the cork exercise. This is a great way to get everyone to know each other *and* warm up their voices at the same time.

Topics

1. What was your favorite childhood game?
2. When you were growing up, what did your bedroom look like?
3. What is your favorite vacation place?
4. If you could travel anywhere, where would it be?
5. What were you like as a kid?
6. Where was your family from originally? What traditions do you still keep?
7. Where were you born? Where did you grow up? What was your hometown like?
8. Have you ever seen a ghost?
9. What is the scariest thing you've ever done, or ever seen?
10. Where are you in the line of siblings (youngest, middle, an only child)? How has this affected you?
11. Who is your favorite actor and why?
12. What was the name of your childhood best friend and what were you like together?
13. If you could live anywhere in the world where would that be and what would you do?
14. Do you like animals or do you have animals? Talk about them if you do.
15. Are you drawn to any particular period, and if so, why? (e.g., the Renaissance, the 1920s, the 1950s).
16. Did you have a favorite subject in school? What was it, and why did you like it?
17. What is the meanest thing someone's ever done to you?
18. What is the nicest thing someone's ever done for you?

19. Up to this point, what is the accomplishment you are most proud of?

20. Is there a movie you could watch over and over again? What is it and why?

21. What type of music do you listen to? Who is your favorite singer, song, band, and why?

22. What do you think happens after we die?

23. What do you think of manners today?

24. What do you think of social media?

25. What is something we no longer do as a society that you think we should bring back?

26. If you have a certain type of nightmare, what is it?

27. Is there any famous figure from any time period you would like to talk to? What would you talk about?

28. How do you feel when you wake up in the morning? Optimistic? Tired? Stressed? Happy?

29. What is your morning routine? What must you do to start your day?

30. What is your nighttime routine? What must you do to end your day?

31. What is one quality in a person you admire that you try to emulate?

32. What is something the people in this class would never guess about you?

33. As an adult, if you could advise the younger you (at any age), what advice or encouragement would you give?

34. What is the most surprising thing you've found out about your parents?

35. Do you have any fears (e.g., spiders, heights)?

36. Is there any celebrity (alive or dead) that you admire? Why?

37. If you could live anywhere in the world where would that be?

38. If you could have another career or job, what would that be?

39. What is your favorite hobby or sport?

40. If you could either fly or be invisible, which would you choose and why?

41. What was your favorite subject in school and why?

42. Are you a morning person or a night person?

43. What does your name mean? Where does it come from?

44. What is your favorite form of exercise and what does it do for you?

45. What is your favorite food and why?

46. Do you like to cook? If yes, what? If no, why?

47. What do you listen to in the car (or on a walk)? If nothing, talk about that.

Facilitate Whole-Person Growth

When ensemble members are aware of positive aspects and places for growth, they will be engaged and inspired. But when individuals seem to be only focusing on themselves in class or rehearsal, try the exercises below.

Names on Paper

This exercise encourages people to get out of their head and into a second circle mindset with the group.

- Write everyone's name on a small piece of paper and put the pieces of paper in a hat or bowl.
- Have everyone pull a name. (If they pick their own name, they should put it back and choose again.)
- Performers should not share whose name they received.
- Each performer remains aware of their person for the entire session.
- At the end of the session, everyone stands in a circle and shares the positive things they noticed about their person. I suggest limiting it to one minute to allow everyone a turn without taking up too much time.

Shake It Up: Directions to Get Started

It's not unusual for improvisers to show up in the same way every week. The characters they play might vary, but their demeanor in class, how they receive notes, and even where they sit can always benefit from a new direction. This exercise can help disrupt those patterns. The goal here is to draw performers' attention to their habitual patterns and inspire them to be curious about what they bring to the classroom and whether it's helpful or not.

- Print out cards (see below) and place them in separate envelopes with a performer's name on each envelope. Place them outside the rehearsal room.
- Performers should be told in advance, "Next time, do not enter the room until you've opened your envelope and read all of the directions."
- In the written directions, performers are instructed to enter the room in character as it is described on the card and to stay in that assigned character until directed otherwise.

- Ideally each performer's roles should be a stretch for them. If they are always the first to get up or tend to talk first, the Healer would be a good one for them. If they tend to sit in the back row or keep to themselves, the In-the-Thick-of-It card would be a good choice.
- Start the exercise with the hosts answering the door as each guest arrives.
- Performers can use their real name but should take on the thinking and behavior of their character.
- The performers mingle onstage in this party atmosphere for around 10–15 minutes.
- Even when you shift into a regular rehearsal, ensemble members should try to maintain the thinking and behavior of their character. Warm up and let everyone experience this new lens. If you shift into scenes, they can play any character needed for the scene, but otherwise they should watch scenes and receive notes from their assigned character's perspective.
- This can keep going for as long as you like but make sure to leave time to share observations and thoughts out of character before the end. How did it feel to play their assigned character? What felt new and exciting? If anyone was uncomfortable, they should be encouraged to explore this, see where it might be prodding them to grow, and try using this new awareness to intentionally change how they show up each week.

Here are the index cards to be assigned to the different participants.

Host A: You love parties, and you love these people. Have a wonderful time with all of them.

Host B: (There can be one or two hosts, depending on the number of participants.) This is your party, and you love everyone here. All is going well at your party. You are not nervous at all.

The Connector: You see connections in everyone and everything. Everything makes sense. All is right and good in your world.

The Healer: You bring a sense of peace and calm wherever you go. You "hold space" at the party for others to feel safe within.

The Helper: Whatever is needed, you are there to lend a helping hand.

The Curious One: You love figuring things out. You are always observing others and are adept at understanding what they mean. People adore you.

The Cheerleader: You love these people and love to play. You are always the first to volunteer for anything.

The Giver: You are always giving comfort or encouragement to those around you. You love to make people feel special.

In the Thick of It: If there is fun around, you are in! You make everything better.

The Eye of the Storm: Sit near others, and with your breath quietly and calmly ground the room and everyone within.

The Cozy-Comfort One: This party is full of people who know you and accept you exactly as you are. There's nothing to prove here—just enjoy yourself with the people you love.

The Playful Sprite: You love to play with people and joke around. You feel 100 percent at ease with everyone in this group.

The Wise One: You are the most experienced one at this party. All go to you for advice. You are confident in your wisdom.

Show Vulnerability

If you're a teacher, director, or ensemble leader, how do you increase trust and cooperation? Remain present and open to learning. By engaging a beginner's mindset, you become more receptive to new ideas that will keep you fresh. Also make it a habit to check in regularly with your level of vulnerability. When I was at Impro Theatre before the pandemic, we often participated in shows with our students. We wanted to perform well with them or in front of them, but failing to do that was a beautiful teaching opportunity *if* we shared our process. They were there, experienced it with us, and could relate. Just as you tell others to embrace failure, so should you, again and again. You are not perfect, and improv is an imperfect art form. Use your own experience with imperfection and you will have yet another way to connect with students or fellow ensemble members.

Being vulnerable doesn't mean being negative though. In February 2020, during a run of *Tennessee Williams UnScripted* in Los Feliz, I received more texts, calls, emails, and verbal congratulations than I have for any show I've done in my improv career. This feedback was in direct contrast to how I felt *during* the performances. The shows felt like work to me. In one show, improvisers were talking so fast and endowing my character with so much information that I felt I had to scramble to justify and make it work. It felt like doing math all night long. I kept this to myself and just listened to the positive feedback I received. It's always best to just say thank you to compliments after a show even if you felt otherwise. If an audience member had a great time and says, "Great show!" and you say, "I thought it was terrible," it diminishes their experience. The contrast between my inner reality (how it felt to be *in* the show) and the audience's experience of the outer reality (the show I was in) was a valuable reminder. Now, when a student tells me how hard it was to be in a scene I have just enjoyed watching, we can have a productive conversation about the difference between the two realities and how to make peace with this seeming contradiction.

Checking In

Doing a physical check in and close out can be beneficial for your team. When I'm teaching, I post the "Dynamics of Energy" handout below (if we are virtual, I share my screen) and then ask students to check in where they are physically starting as class begins. They don't need to go into details. They just say where they are, for example, "I'm arriving today low negative exhausted." Later they may say, "I started class low negative exhausted, and am leaving class high positive joyful." If someone starts high positive and ends low negative, for example, you can encourage further conversation in the moment or privately if needed.

Dynamics of Energy

High Negative	**High Positive**
angry	invigorated
fearful	confident
anxious	challenged
defensive	joyful
resentful	connected

Low Negative	Low Positive
exhausted	relaxed
burned out	mellow
hopeless	peaceful
defeated	tranquil
depressed	serene

We've looked at how to create a positive experience for your group as a whole. Now let's take a look at what you can do as an individual member of the ensemble to make sure you are bringing your best second circle self to rehearsal or class.

9

MINDFUL AWARENESS TO HELP THE INDIVIDUAL WITHIN THE ENSEMBLE

A second circle student often inspires their teacher and their class. The best example I have is Jason Murphy. The following is an excerpt from the eulogy I gave at his memorial service in 2017.

> *Jason was an inspirational student, and while I knew this at the time, it was only in looking back, that I recognized he was the glue that held the class together. More than anything else, Jason was always curious, and it was an honor to be a teacher and mentor to someone who was more curious and fearless than ego-driven. It is a gift to find a student who allows you to teach them, and it was this mindset that allowed us to get to work. You might think this type of mindset would be the norm in an improv class but it's not. I've been teaching improvisation for decades, and he was by far the most accessible student I have had the pleasure of teaching. Jason came to learn, wanted notes, wanted to get better, and trusted the process.*

Looking back, I am not sure who learned more from whom.

Jason was present for the early stages of Impro Theatre, and he helped define an art form that was new to us. His fearlessness onstage, his willingness to attack genre, his incredible brain that allowed us to delve into the narrative and weave technology into our theater—we, Impro Theatre, owe so much to Jason.

Looking back on that era, I see now that he was my shadow teacher. Whenever a student was struggling, I could pair them with Jason because I knew he would help them grow. When I was introducing something I had just made up, I could put Jason up first knowing that if it failed, we would have a great conversation and learn why, *and if it worked, we would have a great discussion about* why. *He was very articulate, and that fantastic brain of his was a joy to work with.*

In short, Jason lifted up the level in the room. He allowed me to teach him, and he came to class to do the work. Take a look at how to develop the skills that will allow you to show up as a second circle student.

Terrible First Times

As improvisers, we are constantly doing what we do for the first time. No matter how much we rehearse, we consistently find ourselves in the unknown. Having a mental strategy for how we experience uncertainty will help us navigate the current moment. Combining the concept of second circle and Brené Brown's strategy for embracing what she calls "terrible first times" (TFTs) is a great way to build resilience in the face of the unknown. Terrible first times are when you try something that is new to you and you fail or aren't good at it *yet*.

When you are in class or rehearsal and struggling with the new, walk yourself through this process.

- Name it: "I'm in a TFT." Clarity gives you power. When we name and own something, we can effect change.
- Normalize it: This is how *new* feels. You're in a TFT. So instead of thinking "I shouldn't be nervous," or "I'll be better when I know everything," you acknowledge that TFTs can feel scary or uncertain.
- Give it perspective: "I'm in the middle of a TFT. It won't last forever. I don't suck at everything." The scene you were in felt difficult. That was one scene. It doesn't define who you are as an improviser.
- Reality-check your expectations: Are you expecting to be perfect? Do you expect the improvised story you are telling with other fallible human beings to be perfect? What does that even mean? How will you know what perfect is? Does your audience want to see a perfect show? According to something called the *pratfall effect*, making mistakes makes us more likable. Messing up draws people closer to you and makes you more human. If you are a perfectionist, take a deep breath right now.

In the 1990s, when I was a member of Scratch Theatre in San Francisco, we did two shows on the same weekend. We had one show that we felt was definitely better than the other. From our perspective, in the first show everything had come together but the second show had felt rough. I remember feeling slightly embarrassed that it had been so messy. However, I discovered while talking to several audience members who had attended both shows that the messy show had been their favorite. It had been exciting for them to see the problems we got into onstage and how we got out of them. They were much more on the edge of their seats and engaged when they felt no one knew how the story would end. It's important to keep in mind that two realities are happening at the same time: the reality in your head as you perform, and the reality of what your audience is experiencing. Very often those two will not line up. Knowing that there is the inner reality of the performer and the outer reality of the audience can help you relax. Stephen Kearin puts it this way, pointing to his head: "Worst seat in the house."

Giving 100 Percent and Retaining Information

I once had a student confess that he only gave 70 percent in class because if it didn't go well, he could tell himself that it was because he hadn't given it his all. Although this was honest, it was also painful to hear. I'd been giving this student extra energy and focus because I saw he was close to a breakthrough. To discover he was consciously holding back was discouraging. I asked him to commit to giving 100 percent. His wholehearted participation would provide me with clarity while coaching. I understood that his energy might vary from week to week, but the intention needed to be present.

Another way to be a second circle improviser is to stay connected to the work you did the week before and come to class or rehearsal mentally prepared to pick up where you left off. Keeping a notebook and then reviewing it before the next session is very helpful. When you are studying a genre, the homework you do on your own is vital. When you arrive prepared for each session, you allow yourself and the whole group to move forward together. If only a handful of your fellow performers retain the information, it is difficult to move forward in a meaningful way. With focused retention, your group can build a strong foundation from which to improvise a story.

How Do You Experience Getting Notes or Being Side Coached?

What happens to you physically and mentally when you receive feedback from your teacher, director, or fellow performers? What physical manifestation do you feel? What does your head tell you when you receive side coaching? How you respond to redirection is up to you. It's vital to identify what the voice in your head is telling you when you receive notes. Very often we experience shame and are unable to recognize it. We've all experienced that warm wash of shame that makes us feel small and not good enough, that makes us wish we could disappear. When you feel shame, you are being hijacked by your brain's limbic system, which wants you to freeze or take flight.

Why is feedback so hard to receive? We *want* that information to go to the *neocortex* because the neocortex is responsible for learning and thinking about the future. But when we feel threatened, the *amygdala* takes over and prevents the information from getting to the neocortex. Instead, the information goes to the *limbic system*, which is the part of the brain involved in our behavioral and emotional responses. So instead of learning, we go into fight-or-flight mode and feel the need to protect ourselves. This is called an *amygdala hijack*.

This feeling may push us to self-protect, and it can show up in responses like these.

- I'm terrible.
- You're wrong.
- Why didn't *X* get this note too?
- I'm being picked on and publicly shamed.
- Let me explain what I was trying to do.
- You aren't good at your job and you're not even a good improviser.

When you recognize the physical symptoms of shame, you can take a breath before you respond. Your body always responds with a feeling first, which is why we call emotions *feelings*. Shame is egocentric, and it will make your focus go inward. This action keeps your mind busy and can result in your inability to hear feedback. If you bring your awareness back to your breath and breathe to the person giving you notes, you will understand them more clearly. Here's what Tory Eletto says: "Befriend your resistance as it will show up in all the spaces that will set you free."

Chronic Confusion as a Form of Resistance

Notice *when* you get confused. Are you chronically confused by the notes a teacher or director gives you? Chronic confusion can be a smokescreen that enables you to stay stuck and unable to be curious about the feedback you receive. Once in a while being confused is understandable, but pay attention if this is a pattern.

Sometimes it will feel safer to stay in a place of confusion rather than understand the truth. I once had a student who was extremely intelligent and equally intuitive. Even though she asked perceptive questions, she had a habit of pleading confusion, especially around groups of people. Later on she revealed to me that she wasn't confused; she was afraid of telling *her* truth and the power that she held. She wanted to be liked, and being perceived as soft or feeble felt safer than being strong and opinionated. Helping her find the balance between being open to new ideas and holding on to her own perspective helped her break free from chronic confusion.

Being Conscious in Real Life

In improv, recognizing an offer, hearing and understanding its implications, absorbing the nuances, and being aware of your response is crucial. If you aren't doing it daily, how can you expect to do it in class or on the stage?

Pay attention to how you habitually spend your day. You may find that what needs work on the improv stage is what you need to work on in real life.

- Do you need to slow down?
- Do you need to listen more carefully?
- Do you make enough eye contact?
- Do you absorb your surroundings?
- Do you drive with focus?

- Do you tell the truth to yourself and others?
- Do you take in the people around you?

These behaviors help to cultivate a second circle mindset.

Your life will be much fuller if you absorb the moments when they happen rather than letting them pass by in a blur. *Feel* your life as it happens rather than continually trying to *figure it out*. Find some sort of touchstone, something that can become a daily practice that keeps you present in the moment. Your touchstone can be to take a breath, to adjust your spine into second, or to look at your surroundings. Daily practice of second circle will go a long way toward ensuring that awareness is at your fingertips when you're under pressure in the improv environment.

Embracing Uncertainty and Discomfort

As improvisers, we must accept that we can never *really* know what will happen next onstage. A central question in the improviser's training is not how to avoid uncertainty and fear but how to relate to the discomfort produced. The discomfort may show up as

- disappointment when your offer is not accepted or when the story isn't going your way
- embarrassment when you make a perceived mistake
- irritation when your call is blocked, canceled, or misunderstood
- fear when you don't know what to do next

Discomfort is a message that tells us to lean into the situation rather than back away. Stay with uncomfortable feelings rather than abandoning yourself and your ensemble. Trust that if you stay in the moment you will intuitively understand what comes next. The current moment holds a spark of information you can use to say, "Yes, and." Ignoring the spark causes more work for you and your ensemble.

Here are some ways we ignore that spark:

- blocking or canceling a new offer by sticking to your plan and clinging to what you thought was going to happen even though it's no longer applicable to the scene or story
- staying attached to the formula of the genre rather than going with what the moment requires
- hesitating, waffling, or joking to ease the tension when tension is what the story needs

Embracing uncertainty is how we learn to relax when the ground beneath us disappears. Be aware of your tolerance level for discomfort. Staying in discomfort makes us feel vulnerable, and that's where the sweet spot is. Stay in the reality of the current moment and you will see opportunities where before you saw none.

The Four Stages of Learning

Knowing there are natural stages of learning may help you stick it out when you are feeling unsuccessful. I was first made aware of these stages through Carol Hazenfield, one of my first improv teachers. A good teacher helps you recognize your blind spots and supports you throughout the learning stages, and Carol was one of the best.

- *Unconscious incompetence* occurs at the beginning of learning. You don't know what you don't know, and therefore you don't know how bad you are yet. Like all ignorance, this is blissful.

Another critical part of this stage is to see the value of a new skill before you move toward it. If you understand why you need to learn what you are learning, you are more likely to endure the rough patches.

- The next stage, *conscious incompetence*, can be the most painful. When you are conscious of your incompetence, you know your shortcomings and are very aware of how much work lies ahead. At this point you must give yourself credit for your growth—after all, it's only after you've learned the fundamentals that you become aware of your shortcomings. Now you have tools to help you advance your work.

- In the stage of *conscious competence*, students often feel they've reached a plateau and are no longer improving. You make choices that pay off; you know how to add to the narrative and succeed at playing a well-rounded character. During this phase, improvising will probably feel more comfortable. Sometimes consciously competent improvisers think they've stopped growing. When you feel like you've plateaued, competence comes more easily, and you succeed more often. Savor this phase a bit because from then on, learning will come in smaller increments and be even harder to measure.

- *Unconscious competence* is the bliss state where you no longer use your conscious mind to make choices. Your choices might surprise you because they'll come from a deeper place in you. This stage arrives unbidden. The more you think or try, the less likely it is you'll be able to reach this phase of letting go. It involves trusting what you know will be expressed if you stay out of the way. Welcome to the flow, the zone, or the trance state.

The transitions from one stage to the next are seldom smooth; you'll likely be moving through the stages nicely in one area of improv while stumbling around in conscious incompetence in other aspects. Now let's take everything you've learned so far in this book and apply it to longer stories told in a specific style or genre.

PART 3

GENRES TO BRING THIS WORK TO LIFE

I've chosen the following genres to introduce what I hope will be a long and happy improvised narrative life for you. Learning specific genres is invaluable to understanding story structure and getting it in your bones. When you are on your feet improvising a play, you want to have a deep knowledge that you can rely on so that you can relax the nervous system and connect to your ensemble. The time limits of the specific acts—just like a play or film—keep you on track. When you are on a stage with no script in front of a paying audience, you must have agreed-on barriers that will keep you from being self-indulgent or lost.

The genre determines and limits what's possible within a story as its design must include the audience's knowledge and anticipations. You are always welcome to break free from these creative limitations, but like athletes who learn a sport, first discover how to do it well then add your style and break the rules.

The creative limitations of genre create freedom within a context of obstacles. The genre conventions do not inhibit creativity; they inspire it. They force the improviser's imagination to rise to the occasion. You can guide your audience through rich, creative variations to reshape and exceed expectations by giving the audience what it hoped for and more than it could have imagined.

What if your rom-com ends with people remaining single or just friends? Exceptions that grow organically out of an improvised narrative are lovely. First learn the form and then organically break the expected patterns together.

This section of the book includes the structure of an improvised play, film, and television episode. I had twenty-two different genres from which to choose so narrowing it down was quite painful. I want to teach you everything! However, what remains is the best of the best, and it will enable you and your fellow improvisers to get on your feet and try full-length (60–120 minutes), improvised stories for yourselves.

None of these genres will work if your ensemble does not understand how to connect in second circle or a flow state. From there the previous exercises and upcoming genre templates will pave the way to a long, successful, narrative improv adventure.

10

IMPROVISING A THREE-ACT
PLAY IN ONE LOCATION

In this chapter I will take you step-by-step through a template for improvising a full-length play. For this illustration I have chosen the mid-century, Midwestern playwright William Inge. You can select the playwright who inspires you most: August Wilson, Tennessee Williams, Jane Chambers, Lorraine Hansberry, Kunio Kishida, Anton Chekhov, Paula Vogel, Henrik Ibsen, or Tony Kushner, for example.

If you're the director, once you pick your playwright, the work begins. Read everything you can including, if applicable, their short stories. Williams and Chekhov's short stories allowed me to understand their plays more deeply. In fact, I prefer their short stories to their plays. The descriptive locations of Chekhov's Russia came alive. Their character types show up differently, allowing a better understanding of what makes them tick. The director's job is to take on the macro view of the playwright and handpick the (micro) homework for the cast. The materials you provide them with, or that they research on their own, will serve as a lens as they immerse themselves in the world of the playwright you have chosen. What do they need to know about the time period, themes, playwright bio, and learned, societal points of view?

Create Your Play Dossier

A play dossier can be an essential tool to help performers immerse themselves in the world of the playwright and the conventions of their work. It should include the following:

Playwright's Biography and Quotes

These help us understand the playwright's point of view as a writer.

Source Materials

Plays, one-acts, short stories, and so on. You should read everything and then make selections for ensemble members with specific take-aways in mind.

Play Style

This should be a breakdown of nine aspects for your improvised play. Inge was considered a realist playwright. Here are nine possible aspects for your improv.

- Inge's concerns (theme): Inge focused on society and its impact on his characters. The depiction of sociopolitical concerns is an aspect of realism.

- Inge's point of view: His writing style is objective in the sense that the audience is outside the events being depicted and observing them.

- Inge's world: The world Inge creates in his plays is very similar to the real world and easily identified as such.

- Inge's plot construction: The events are in chronological order, and the audience follows along easily.

- The substance or texture of Inge's characters: The characters are three-dimensional with ideas, feelings, personalities, passions, and foibles similar to those of real people.

- Inge's setting: Inge meant his play settings to be tangible and realistic. They stay constant so the audience can focus more on what is happening with the characters.

- Inge's language: Inge's American Midwest language is unadorned and easy to understand. He is a master at using dialect and accent to reflect a setting. Colloquialisms and slang keep the language fresh and real.

- Inge's form: Inge's plays are representational. There is no direct address to the audience, and the fourth wall is intact. The actors don't step outside the world of the play and talk to the audience.

- Inge's definition of the world: Inge uses realism to illustrate the restrictive nature of society's rules and how breaking those rules can lead to a more fulfilling life.

Characters

Inge's cast of characters are, typically, members of a family or a group that functions like a family—longtime coworkers, bar patrons, and so on—who inhabit the same dysfunctional world, some willingly and some unwillingly. Inge's older characters usually feel their best years have passed them by while the younger ones worry they will suffer the same fate unless they *do* something.

When the characters have a specific POV, tension will appear when they are all thrust together. Performers need not create a plot; instead, they need to be someone specific with a POV and let themselves be affected by each other. What archetypes or character types inhabit your playwright's world? It is essential to capture this and have the ensemble on the same page. What are their POVs and wants?

Themes

A playwright writes to explore something important to them. It could be second chances, or death, or love. Inge's plays center on characters with hidden desires, lost innocence, and broken dreams, and the impact of society on these characters. The depiction of sociopolitical concerns is an aspect of realism. These themes should be explored in rehearsal and expressed through characters. Creating POV cards can help to facilitate this exploration.

Setting

The setting is where our story takes place, and it's extremely important to the play. It has an immense effect on the plot and the characters. Furthermore, it can also establish a story's atmosphere or mood. What I love about improvising a play is that we stay in the same location for the entire time. Because of this, the environment is visceral and can affect you deeply, making improvising easier.

Examples of some of Inge's settings include a multigenerational family home (*Picnic*); places where strangers are forced to be together (*Bus Stop*); and an isolated couple's home (*Come Back, Little Sheba*). A description of the setting at the beginning of *Come Back Little Sheba* reads in part,

> At rise of curtain, the sun hasn't come out in full force and outside the atmosphere is a little gray. The house is extremely cluttered and even dirty. The living room somehow manages to convey the atmosphere of the twenties, decorated with cheap pretense at niceness and respectability. The general effect is one of fussy awkwardness. The furniture is all heavy and rounded-looking, the chairs and davenport being covered with a shiny mohair.

What kinds of things do we make up about the inhabitants of such a place? People living in a cluttered, dirty environment may give off a feeling of despair. Maybe at one point this was a nice room, but that was a long time ago. Your improvised setting with details that you verbally endow upon the space can help the audience understand the characters on a much deeper level. Take time to rehearse the location speed-endowment skill at the end of this chapter.

Plot Structure: Linear or Nonlinear?

For our purposes here, there are two plot structures—linear and nonlinear. Inge's play *Picnic* is linear; its events happen in chronological order. Within either linear or non-linear plots, what's referred to as Freytag's pyramid, charts dramatic action in a play.

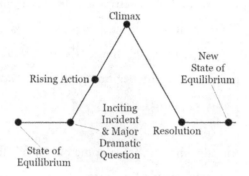

Act 1

The action builds very slowly. The first act should be used to set up the characters' hopes and dreams and give a sense of their past. Show subtext and suppressed emotions like mad throughout this first act. Depicting mundane, everyday tasks are an excellent way to do this—for example, ironing angrily or washing dishes wistfully.

Key aspects of this act are

- state of equilibrium: What is the status quo of the world we are entering?
- inciting incident: What happens to disrupt this world?
- major dramatic question: Will our leads survive? Be found out? Find love?

Act 2

This act delves into the problems at hand but can also present the hope of a solution. The past might seem oppressive, but there are always moments when real joy or hope bursts through.

- rising action: Things are heating up. Will our leads rise to the occasion or make a change in their lives?
- climax: Everything set up in act 1 has exploded. The world is altered.

Act 3

In the final act, the revelation of devastating truths destroys lives. For some, the will to survive endures.

- resolution: Truths are revealed, and change is possible.
- A new state of equilibrium: We go back to the beginning, and our leads either put their heads back in the sand or leave the play's world.

Additional Material

The show dossier should include information so that ensemble members can familiarize themselves with the following.

- historical information leading up to this era
- cost of living
- common occupations
- politics
- gender roles
- education
- food
- clothing
- transportation
- entertainment

- inventions
- names commonly used

Steep yourself in the work in between shows. Read aloud, look at pictures from the era, do whatever inspires you. When you stand in front of an audience and improvise in a genre, you are telling the audience that you know this genre or playwright so well that you can make up plays in this style.

For Your Technical Improvisers

The following are the kinds of material your technical improvisers will need to prepare and rehearse.

Music

What music suits the beginning, closing, and transitions?

- walkout song: Have a song that sets the tone from when the actors walk out onstage. This can also be used after the final bow.
- first scene: For an Inge play, once the initial suggestion or suggestions are provided by the audience and the lights come down, I use "The Owens Family," from the soundtrack for the movie version of *The Picnic*. It sets the tone for small-town America. Pick what's right for *your* play.
- In Inge's plays, there are often characters that reference music nearby. Have dancing music from the correct era ready if they turn on the radio or record player. The sound of someone

practicing the piano would be good to have. Also, marching bands or parades are very important in small-town America.

When you read your playwright's work, make lists of sounds you can collect.

Lights

What mood do you wish to create with lighting?

- Since you stay in the same location, keep the lights up for the first act and let the actors come in and out of the primary area as needed. After establishing the first act, you can bring lights up and down as needed.
- Set playing areas on the stage for the actors in advance. These are intentionally lit areas that the improvisers know to go to; for example, downstage center, downstage left, and downstage right. If you don't set these areas, improvisers will stand in the center of the stage and talk. Use the nine *X*s in chapter 3 and set the stage for your improvised play with powerful improvised blocking.

Scenes

Explore the length of scenes, acts, and transitional lighting and sound. In *Come Back Little Sheba*, there are six scenes in two acts.

- act 1, scene 1: A morning in late spring.
- act 1, scene 2: The same evening after supper.

- act 2, scene 1: The following morning.
- act 2, scene 2: 5:30 p.m. the same day.
- act 2, scene 3: The next morning.
- act 2, scene 4. A morning a week later.

(Note: very little time passes in these plays. We have also found that a three-act structure is easier to improvise.)

Exercises for Rehearsal

POV Cards

Write down POVs that are appropriate to characters in an Inge play on index cards and have each actor pick one before starting their scene. As in previous exercises, have the actors choose a blue-taped X and sculpt themselves according to the POV on their card (see chapter 3). Rehearse your play this way for as long as possible to get good stage blocking and body placement in your bones. These POVs will help you create your playwright's type of characters.

First Lines

Go through plays from the playwright and write down random lines on index cards. Have an improviser pick a card and say the line. Use these as scene starts for your improvised scenes in the rehearsal period.

Here are some random lines from actual Inge plays.

- "Dreams are funny."
- "Let's not talk about it anymore."
- "Habits change. Here's your fruit juice."

- "I mean, are you sorry you had to marry me?"
- "Sometimes, I feel sorta proud of myself."
- "I had another dream last night."
- "I wanted to, but you wouldn't let me."

Note how lines like these can launch you into a scene quickly.

Speed-Endow the Environment

This exercise will help improvisers describe a location by warming up the muscle needed to endow the environment at the beginning of your improvised play.

- Pair improvisers up and scatter them throughout the room.
- Each pair decides who will start. This will be person A.
- Person B gives person A a location to describe, which might be the setting of a made-up play—a laundromat, a living room, the deck of a boat, or an attic, for example.
- Set a timer for two minutes.
- Person A describes the made-up environment as if they are *in* the environment. They should move around the location and touch the things they mention.
- At the end of two minutes, person B will prompt person A.
- Set your timer for another two minutes. The prompts are
  - solid mass: What are the walls like in this space? What material is on the floor? How high is the ceiling? Describe it.
  - texture: Is there texture in the room? Wood, metal, fabric? Describe and touch it.
  - light: Where are the light sources in the room? Is it natural or human-made? Where are the shadows?

- color: Is there a predominant color in the room? What colors are here?
- sound: What sounds do you hear in the room and outside the room?
- For one more minute, person B gets to ask any questions about the space just described if it's still unclear in their mind.
- Now switch. Person B guides person A in this made-up location, adding details to what was mentioned or filling out areas that were missed.
- At the end of the exercise, when both sides have gone (five minutes each), have the pairs reflect on the following:
  - What types of details stick in your mind about the locations described?
  - What type of people might inhabit the space you created?
  - How might we explore this environment in the first act of our made-up play?

Improvise in These Locations

Keep the same pairs as you did above and now do scenes in these made-up locations. They spent so much time describing them—what happens when they live in them for a while? The endowed environment creates character behaviors that are interesting to explore.

In Closing

Any of the exercises introduced in this book will help you in your improvised play rehearsals. The trifecta of the playwright's POV, your

POV, and the artform of improv will create a one-of-a-kind play that will never be seen again. How brave to let the world experience your first draft!

In an improvised play, your locations are minimal and the scenes are longer. Let's build on this skill and shift to an improvised teleplay that will require shorter scenes and more locations.

11

IMPROVISED TELEVISION
NIGHTTIME SOAP OPERA

I grew up watching *Dynasty*, *Dallas*, and *Falcon Crest*, so bringing the essence of these shows to the stage combined with 1980s hair and fashion is a pure delight. The soap opera genre teaches stage blocking and strong scene-enders like no other. Taking all of the tips from this book and getting the elements of second circle and soap opera blocking into your ensemble's bones is imperative before attempting to improvise this genre on the stage.

Soap operas have been a staple of the television world since they first gained traction in the 1950s. However, it wasn't until the 1980s that the prime-time soap opera was born. While a daytime soap aired every weekday and was usually targeted to an audience of housewives and college students, prime-time soaps only aired once a week, during prime-time hours. Prime-time soaps also targeted a wider audience; however, they still retained the drama and shocking plot twists that make soap operas so appealing.

The soap opera is a serial narrative. It is a story told through a series of individual, narrative-linked installments. Soaps are often set in a fictitious place and centralized around two or three well-to-do families.

This genre is unusual for improvisers in that we know our characters in advance and get to inhabit them once a week until the end of the run of shows. This can be a refreshing change as you get to live in your character's shoes for a while and know them intimately. At the end of an improvised season of soap, you can look back at your story line and be amazed at where you ended up.

As the director of an improvised soap, I work with the actors and we create characters for them that are sometimes out of their comfort zone if they want to try something new. As a teaching tool, this is valuable because if they tend toward only playing nice characters, they will have an opportunity to rehearse and perform in the shoes of a villain. They can have a breakthrough in their work while having fun at the same time.

The show will have energy and be fun if you do it earnestly or in a campy spirit. There's no room in this genre for mild, casual performances. Here's Arlo Sanders's take on soaps.

> Getting cast to play the villain in soap was extremely beneficial
> for me as an actor. It taught me how to play someone who is
> the complete opposite of myself and live in it. I worked on my
> character for several months and what I learned in the process
> was that bad guys don't think of themselves as evil; they just
> want something so much that they are willing to do anything
> to get it. They are real human beings with hurts and desires.
> My villain was motivated by lost love, and it drove him to

be the way he was. When I was able to empathize with my character, I could rationalize his behavior and attitude toward others.

Doing this work expanded my range as a performer. I used to have a hard time tapping into the villain, and I was uncomfortable playing someone cruel. It's now an archetype I feel very comfortable playing because of all the work and discovery I put into the process. It makes me genuinely believe that as actors we can become a blank canvas for any type of character no matter who we are. Soap gave me the tools, the brushes, and paint to color my canvas with a fully fleshed-out character.

Classic Prime-Time Soap Story Lines and Themes

- a power struggle over a family fortune
- a love triangle
- young love
- unrequited love
- rekindled love
- good twin versus evil twin
- dating on the wrong side of the tracks
- Who's the father of the baby?
- the stranger in town with a secret past
- the return of a character who was presumed dead or missing
- forced into a secluded situation with nemesis
- amnesia and comas
- a murder, a trial, who done it, the wrongly accused

Characters

Characters in prime-time soaps are often driven by a single objective that doesn't allow them to change as a character until that objective comes to fruition. They will seldom undergo a dramatic change in perspective unless directly observing something; for example, catching their lover with someone else or overhearing a plot against them. There are many types of characters with a variety of wants, but these are three staples of the nighttime soap.

- The super couple. Soaps thrive on a super couple story line and are most exciting when a fan-favorite couple is in an epic battle to save their relationship whether threatened by status, family disapproval, or, more often than not, a classic love triangle.
- The hero. Soaps are ensemble story lines, but often there will be one good person who is tormented by the soap's villain.
- Villains. Villains can be as popular as heroes because an audience can love to hate them, but it's the hero's triumph over all obstacles that keeps the audience tuning in.

Want

Soap characters want something so badly they will risk anything to get it. When you are developing your characters, make sure to have various good and evil characters in the cast. Take a look at this list of the seven deadly sins and see what kind of character inspires you.

- pride or vanity
- envy or jealousy

- wrath or anger
- sloth or laziness
- avarice or greed
- gluttony
- lust

Scene Starts and Endings

Scene Starts

Soap opera blocking is essential for scene starts and throughout as the scene progresses. Knowing the power position of your character, their status, and their emotional state will guide you into where and how to place yourself onstage. Let your body lead rather than your head. Refer to the blocking exercises in chapter 3. The X grid is key for learning soap opera blocking.

The start of any given scene is often the continuation of an ongoing story line. The relationship between the people in the scene should be defined immediately as it is rare that a soap scene will start with two strangers.

Scene Endings

Knowing when to end a scene is key to the soap genre because every scene ending is essentially where the next scene between those two characters will begin. Scenes can end a number of different ways.

End with a Question

A scene-ending question is directly related to the central story line and can be asked in every way possible before it is ever answered.

Scene-ending questions are often in two parts. Here's an example: "Why didn't you tell me Felipe was in town? What else aren't you telling me?" Now lights out, and you will pick up from there. Don't answer it yet!

End with a Decision

Where you are headed, what's the plan, what's your next move? This lets the audience as well as your scene partners know what scene should come next: "I'm going to see the mayor right now." Decisions can accompany the performer exiting the stage.

End with an Opportunity

This scene ending is meant to challenge the character receiving the opportunity and is commonly used by villains. It may promise seduction, money, or power. Here's an example: "Help me, Jamal, and all of Montgomery Enterprises will be yours."

End with a Threat

"If you walk out that door I'll tell all of Hope Falls the truth about who you really are." Using a threat can help a character get their way. It's a classic scene ender.

End with a Reveal

Reveals can be tricky and should only be made to drive the story line, not end it. A big reveal shouldn't come until the final episode, but little reveals are essential as they show character. For villains, reveals can be an excellent manipulation tool. They tell just enough to keep the story line moving but not the big picture.

small reveal: "I saw you leave the scene of the accident."

big reveal: "You thought I was dead, but you were wrong."

With the verbal scene enders above, you can stop talking and look out over the audience while your technical improvisers bring the lights down and bring the music to a swell.

Instead of ending a scene verbally, you can also practice actions that will help bring the lights down.

End with Being Caught in the Act

Another classic ending is when someone enters your scene and catches you having an affair, stealing money, standing over a body, or something similar.

End with a New Character Entrance

It's often at the end of a scene that a new character makes their entrance. The audience may be unsure whether they're a hero or a villain. When you enter, you should say your full name or someone else should. For example,

Rosie: Who are you?

Cassandra: I'm Cassandra. Cassandra Drake. (Cassandra turns to the audience; music sting; lights fade)

Soap opera story lines may vary in how much they build up a new character in advance. Often there's a lengthy build-up: two or three scenes with pick-ups (see below) where you describe who they are and allude to what purpose they will serve in the story. The new character can be rumored to be in town, or you may have a meeting with them in a few hours. New characters can also appear with little build up in a location, where they sit at a bar or in a coffee shop, and we hear two characters have a conversation about who that person is. After a pick-up or two, the new character can interact with the other characters in the scene.

Two types of new characters deserve special mention.

- **the love interest entrance:** When characters are brought on as love interests, we should feel the spark even if those characters are at odds.
- **the new hero entrance:** The hero rushes in to help an established character in a scene. They might save them from an accident, or if they are the doctor, step into their hospital room.

Special Types of Scenes

Flashback Scenes

There are several reasons you might want to introduce a flashback scene. You might want to show the reason behind a character's present state of mind; to recall happier memories between two lovers; or to say something about someone who has died. Effective flashback scenes typically include verbal as well as technical cues.

Verbal flashbacks: "I remember the accident like it was yesterday"; "We were so happy then"; "I know he's gone, but I feel his presence still."

Technical flashbacks: the lights start flashing, the music swells. The actors on the stage spin slowly and land in the past, do a short scene, then slowly spin back to the present.

Monologues

A monologue allows you to go deeper into a character's current state of mind and give the audience history and emotion to clarify who that character is and how that character feels about others in the story. There are two classic soap monologues to practice.

- **inner monologues said out loud:** Whenever you're alone onstage, go ahead and talk to yourself. In soap, your innermost thoughts, plots, and emotions are said aloud so the audience and your fellow improvisers can hear what you're thinking.
- **Emmy-winning monologues:** When you're in a scene, know when it's time to monologue. Your scene partner might set you up for this, or you may realize you've just said a line that's perfect for delving deeper into your emotions. This would be the clip your agent sends that gets you nominated for your Emmy. It is high-stakes emotions expressed out loud, downstage, in your light.

Sample Show Structure

The key to this genre is the pick-up rule: Do three scenes with your scene partner or partners in the first act then move on to another location and new scene partners in the second act and again new scene partners and location for the third act. For example, my character Olivia Montgomery in our improvised soap *Avalon Terrace* might do three scenes with the mayor, Jimmy Peeples, in the first act; three scenes with her twin sister in the second act; and three scenes with her mother, Erica Montgomery, in the third act. If you keep this in mind while watching a real soap opera, you may notice this pattern.

The scenes in an improvised first act tend to be shorter because we need momentum to start the show. You end your scene with one of the scene enders above (question, decision, opportunity, threat, reveal), and you pick up in the next scene exactly where you left off. For an improvised, one-hour soap opera, this might be your timeline.

Act 1 (0–20 minutes): Lift! Show us the world.

Act 2 (20–40): Go deeper into the world you've created.

Act 3 (40–55): End the show with high stakes so the audience tunes in next week!

(When my ensemble does soap opera episodes, we often have to start a few minutes late, and there are shows right after us in the theater, so we usually end up doing fifty-minute shows. Our cast sizes range between eight and ten improvisers.)

Vary tone between scenes. If the current scene is dark, go light in the next one. If the current scene is stationary, be physical in the next one. Make sure to vary the scenes with solo monologues, duos, group scenes, action, sweet moments, and so on.

Make sure your scenes are about something and state what you want. You get three shots at your scene, each round progressing just a little further. Go deeper into your second round, and it will build nicely to the third.

1980s Homework

As we saw in chapter 10, it's important that the performers familiarize themselves within the era. Assign these topics and any others you are interested in and have every ensemble member report back what they learn.

- fashion
- cost of living
- occupations
- politics
- roles of women
- roles of men
- education
- food
- transportation
- entertainment
- inventions

For Your Technical Improvisers

Pre-Show Music

If you're in the 1980s, for example, use upbeat romantic-themed music from that decade.

Previously On

The song that plays on a loop during your previously on section (where you recap what happened in the previous episode) is key in that it sets a tone. Check out the "Timber Falls Theme" by Henning Lohner.

Underscoring

Music that underscores each scene to support tone and suspense is vital to a show's success. Check out these songs and discover what works best for your show.

- "Fondly" (Kerry Muzzey—my favorite!)
- "The Betrayal" (Kerry Muzzey)
- "Sacrifice" (Kerry Muzzey)
- "Suspension" (Kerry Muzzey)
- "Countdown to Destruction" (Kerry Muzzey)
- "Iron" (instrumental mix; AtcG)
- "Secrets of James Bond and Ian Fleming Ch. 9" (O. H. Krill)
- "Rhythm Studios N. 01" (Jeroen and Sandra Van Veen)
- "Evil's Suite: Through the Earth" (Corviria)
- "Fall into the Dreamscape" (Static Syndrome)
- "Lights" (Catalynx)
- "Senorita" (Brooklyn Duo)
- "Voices" (Cloudwalker remix; Attractive Deep Sound)

Bow Music

As the performers bow at the end of the show, have a repeat of your opening theme as the voiceover says, "Join us next week for another episode of . . ."

Lights

I like to define playing areas that the improvisers can go to. Generally I like the middle of the stage open while downstage right there will be two chairs that can go from being a car to a restaurant to an office. Downstage left we usually have a settee that could be a bed, a living room, or the back of a car. These playing areas are lit with specials so the general stage lights can go out and direct our eyes and focus our attention.

Physical Action

There are certain physical actions that are familiar features of soap operas but they have to be carefully rehearsed with the full consent of everyone involved and with safety prioritized above all else. It's best to involve professional fight choreographers or intimacy coordinators if your performers are not already trained in these areas.

Fights

There is an infamous catfight in a fountain between the two female leads in an episode of *Dynasty*. Moments like this can be very fun and enliven the stage and story, but obviously they can be dangerous if not planned and rehearsed thoroughly. Keep the following in mind.

- A professional stage combat instructor might be needed to work with your group.
- Slowing down, making eye contact, maintaining communication, and seeing the fight as a dance are key aspects to stage-fighting safely. If you are stage fighting, you need to be in tune (in second circle) with the other performer.
- Even if a hit looks really fake, it'll work. Having realistic stage combat in an improv show isn't as exciting as you may think. It

makes the audience nervous. Take care of your audience. Don't pull them out of the show by making them uncertain if you are in control of your body.

Slaps

They're a trope of this genre, but think about whether it's really necessary to fake-slap another performer. At a minimum, performers should be clear about whether they're okay with this. Fake slaps should be carefully rehearsed.

Kisses

There was a time we could put our lips together at the end of a scene and know the lights would come down immediately. Things have changed now and not everyone is comfortable with this. Instead of kissing, your romantic leads can simply embrace before the lights go down. Have a clear discussion on comfort levels and create workarounds that everyone feels good about.

Car Chases

Car chases (see chapter 12) can be an interesting element to introduce to a soap. The physical energy will give variety to what might otherwise be a talky genre. To build on this idea, let's shift from an improvised soap to an improvised film in the buddy action genre.

12

OPPOSITES ATTRACT

BUDDY ACTION STORIES

Buddy action (buddy cop) stories are in some ways similar to rom-coms. I like the opposites-attract element of many rom-coms, and there are buddy action films that handle this dynamic very well. It's helpful to think about them as a relationship genre combined with an action genre. The chemistry between the two buddies is everything, and it usually ends with them feeling (platonic) love and appreciation for each other. In my opinion, our society leans too hard on romantic love, and exploring friendship is much more interesting and appealing to me.

I call this genre *buddy action* and not *buddy cop* because my favorite style is when a cop is paired with a non-cop. The best example of this is *Midnight Run*. Please watch this film for inspiration.

I used to provide a list of buddy action films for my students to watch for research. These days I can no longer with a clear conscience assign the classic films of this genre for homework. There is so much misogyny and racism inherent in the genre that I cannot tell you to go watch them! However, improvising within this genre, you have the opportunity to create a much more inclusive film. The genre can use your help.

One note about language and speech patterns in this genre: the dialogue should be quippy and light-hearted even in the face of danger. If one or more characters is a police officer, a great resource for learning terminology and slang is the book *Cop Speak: The Lingo of Law Enforcement and Crime* by Tom Philbin.

Finally, fight scenes are often a feature of the buddy action genre, but they have to be rehearsed extensively and carefully. Refer to the guidelines on fight scenes in chapter 11.

Characters

Leads

The essence of buddy action stories is that two very different people have to work together. Classic examples include *Midnight Run* ("a bounty hunter pursues a former Mafia accountant who is also being chased by a rival bounty hunter, the FBI, and his old mob boss after jumping bail"); and *Lethal Weapon* ("a straight-laced LAPD detective teams up with an unhinged cop who, distraught after his wife's passing, has a death wish and takes unnecessary risks").

Opposite personality traits or competing objectives work beautifully to create tension that will propel you through your improvised story. The key point is that the two leads are stuck together for the story's duration. Don't let up on this premise as it will drain the narrative of its momentum.

At the heart of the story is a case or other problem that the two protagonists have to work together to solve. Conflict is inherent between the two at the beginning, but throughout the story they grow to understand each other. The key to this genre is the relationship between the two leads and not the case or problem that brings them together.

Almost always one or both of the leads is a police officer or detective. A traditional pairing, as in *Lethal Weapon*, brings together two officers who are vastly different in personality, style, and work habits but are forced together by their superiors. When I do this type of buddy action story, we either improvise a backstory between the two that makes them not like each other or we have a scene where each reveals why they act the way they do. We usually start with a crime and then introduce the buddies separately before they are put together on the case.

In a movie like *Midnight Run*, a police officer is made to work with someone who is not a member of the force. An expert, a lawyer, a private investigator, a witness, a kid, an animal, or maybe even a criminal could all be tapped for this role.

With this approach, we typically have the cop give early on a reason why they dislike the second kind of individual—and then, of course, they are forced to work together. To start, we ask for an occupation or identity for the partner from the audience. In the first scene we meet the cop and get to know them before they're paired up with the civilian for a specific reason—the civilian might have an expertise that will be needed to solve the crime, for example.

In either style, the leads need to have opposing traits to play with, which can be requested from the audience as a suggestion. For example,

- anxious versus relaxed
- efficient versus a daydreamer
- meticulous versus haphazard
- controlling versus chaotic
- carefree versus a perfectionist
- orderly versus sloppy
- logical versus faith-based
- easily distracted versus focused
- hedonistic versus highly disciplined

It's important that each person use their unique abilities to help the investigation as the story progresses.

Secondary Characters

For a story that involves the police, other cast members may include

- **the commander or chief:** The chief should give the reason why the case is especially important. They can also give the leads a deadline, and they should stay involved (in person or via radio) during the whole story to keep up the pressure and even raise the stakes or tighten a deadline.
- **the snitch:** a character who reveals key information about the case.
- **the witness:** an innocent bystander who may become romantically involved with one of the leads. The witness later may reveal that they are more than they appear.
- **other officers:** Additional police officers can help to move the story along.

- **the possibly dirty cop:** This is another officer in the department who acts either suspiciously or seems too helpful. If they are helpful, they generally turn out to be bad. If they are suspicious, they usually end up helping the investigation.
- **the cop's friends and family:** These are people who help to show the cop's personal life. These people sometimes also end up in harm's way.

Villains

Villains are over-the-top evil. They have no morals and no compunction about torturing or killing people. They can also show a false, nice side, and their switching between the two makes them fun to play and watch. They usually have a front company or other location that they use to disguise their hideout or base of operations.

Flesh out your villain. Clarify their goals, desires, and reasons for being the way they are. Try to do this early in act 2. Remember, though, that we can always learn there's more to what they're up to even near the end. In movies like *Die Hard* or *Lethal Weapon*, the villain's actual plan or motivation is revealed near the climax. Also bear in mind that during act 2 or even 3 it's very cool if things can be made personal between the villain and one or both of the leads!

The villain should maintain one or more sidekicks, who can help by having expositional dialogue with the villain. Familiar types include the sycophant, the bungler, the meaner-than-the-devil tough guy, and so on.

A great way to practice slowing down and giving your audience a bit of background on your villain is by rehearsing the talisman monologue (see chapter 4). During rehearsal, assign your villain an imaginary object to hold in their hands, facing the audience downstage in a pool of light. Ask them to do a 1–2 minute monologue about why this object is important to their character. It can be anything—a pen, a snow-globe, a lighter. Their job is to make it important and help us understand why. The sidekicks can be in this scene too, listening.

Three Act Structure

The following provides a structure for an *overly directed* buddy action story. This structure can be helpful as you begin rehearsals, but you should plan on eventually letting this exact scene order go. These are training wheels. Once the ensemble is on the same page, you can be freer with the structure and find new things in each show. Your buddy action story should not feel the same every time.

Act 1 (15–25 Minutes)

- A crime is committed or discovered in a scene that is usually brief and mysterious. The villain usually does not appear and is not involved at this stage. The crime should be a serious one, such as a murder or robbery, even if that's not apparent in this first scene. It may become bigger later in the story as more is revealed about what's going on.
- We meet lead 1 in their usual environment.
- We meet lead 2 in their usual environment.
- The chief puts the leads together on the case, explaining why it's urgent and often gives a deadline.

- Our buddies drive to the crime scene and get on each other's nerves.
- At the crime scene, another officer gives the leads a basic rundown of what has happened and helps to flesh out the location. The buddies look for clues in a way that's true to their personality traits, and eventually they find one together that sends them off in a new direction.

Remember: The story is all about the buddies' relationship. Pump it up to eleven from the start, which gives you the most room for their attitudes toward each other to change later on.

Act 2 (20–30 Minutes)

- We usually open on the villain at their hideout or front company interacting with one or more sidekicks in a way that brings out the villain's character and objectives.
- We see the buddies at whatever location the clue in act 1 has led them to. There they figure something out that gets them a step closer to the villain and the plot.

The rest of act 2 is loose but can include the following elements.

- The villain keeps winning or outmaneuvering the buddies through most of the act if not all of it.
- The buddies still dislike each other despite being impressed by what they see or learn about each other.
- The chief stays involved to add pressure and raise the stakes. Often the chief calls in the buddies and grills them for messing

something up. The chief then threatens to take them off the case, suspend them and take their guns and badges, or demote them to patrol or desk duty—or the chief actually does one of these things. The buddies argue and blame each other, but since the chief blames them both as a team, they naturally start to bond.

- Family and friend characters continue to play a role to keep the buddies' personal lives in the story.
- We're given a why-I'm-like-this monologue. In a moment of rage—usually during a stakeout—one or both of the buddies prompts the other to explain why they are the way they are. This launches a monologue that fleshes out the buddies' backstories and draws them closer. It may be interrupted with a high-energy event like a shoot-out or chase.

Here's how to practice this type of monologue.

- Pair everyone up around the room.
- Partner A gives partner B a character trait—for example, hot-headed, peaceful, jumpy, or resigned.
- Partner A launches into a monologue about why they have this particular trait.
- Then the partners switch.

To bring act 2 to a close, keep the following in mind.

- A cliff-hanger should end the act. Maybe a piece of information comes to light that sends the case in a new direction, or a key piece of information from earlier is found out to be a lie, or someone important is kidnapped, or the buddies are captured, or the buddies think they've wrapped up the case only to discover they were wrong and it's far bigger than they thought.

- Putting someone we care about in peril is always effective.
- If a big clue went unexplained or big question unanswered in act 1, here's where we figure it out.

Act 3 (8–12 Minutes)

- Here the buddies track down the villain—if they haven't already at the end of act 2.
- This is the climax. The resolution of all the plot threads should come just in time to solve the case and save the day so that the bad guys get their due.
- One or both of the buddies will use their partner-buddy's character traits to save the day. For example, the by-the-book cop will break down a door without a warrant and stop the bad guys who are about to shoot their way to freedom. During the climax, the two buddies are a dynamic team, brilliant together.

Coda

- The final scene, often back in the chief's office, wraps up any loose ends and caps the buddies' character arcs. Any location will work if it's significant to this specific story.
- At this point it's great to bring in anyone we cared about from the buddies' personal lives.

Chases

There are many styles of chases. All should be rehearsed carefully and with emphasis on the performers' safety. The two below are ones that I've found especially effective to work into the buddy action genre.

Seven-Part Foot Chase

At the beginning, exciting music is playing *loudly*.

- A sidekick comes on, running from the cops and creating the layout of the location with their movements: ducking, leaping, climbing, and so on.
- The buddies chase the sidekick through the same location, performing the same physical movements to navigate the space.
- The lights and focus shift to a fourth character in another location doing an *unrelated* activity such as a groomsman giving a toast or a child reciting a poem in front of a classroom.
- The focus shifts back to the sidekick in a new location and again describing a new environment through movements such as rowing, crawling, ducking, leaping, and climbing.
- Again the buddies chase the sidekick through the new location and make the same physical movements.
- A fourth person picks up their scene in the same location, staying onstage as the sidekick and buddies race into that location for the climax of the chase.
- At this point the music softens so we can hear the actors in the scene.

Car Chase

- Generally the way that onstage car chases work is that you have the leads seated in one car either pursuing or being chased by the villain's or sidekick's car. The cars do not actually move.

- I have found that lightweight chairs are the best to use as cars. Have two chairs for the buddy car on one side, and two others for the villain van or car on the other side. If the character is on a motorcycle, they can just crouch and mime the action of riding (similar to riding a horse) while tech or someone with a microphone makes sound effects.

- If you can isolate the cars with focused lighting keeping the rest of the stage dark, that's ideal.

- Work closely with your techs on lights and sound during the rehearsal process until everyone is clear on how to make this a very exciting part of the show.

Technical Improvisation

Specific Scenes

The scenes in a buddy action story tend to be shorter and the locations much more varied than in, say, a realistic play. The following tips work well with the three-act structure outlined above.

- After the suggestion is received from the audience, bring the lights down and bring up the volume of the genre music. Give the stage very dark, atmospheric lighting. The first scene is fairly short. We see the crime and don't know much of anything yet.

- In the next scenes we'll meet the buddies. Based on the crime and the buddies' personality traits, ideally the tech team will have already been thinking about what underscoring the buddy scenes may need. If "obsessed with cleanliness" is a trait picked, then maybe classical music would be a good choice. If the trait "slob" was picked, chaotic music might work well.
- In chase scenes—foot or car—and fight scenes, quick, light cues and loud music will help sell all of it. This needs to be rehearsed extensively ahead of time.

Sound

- Before the show begins, immerse the waiting audience in wonderful, energized, 1980s music (or music appropriate to whatever time period you've chosen).
- Underscoring scenes is a huge part of this genre. You can use preexisting music, or you may want to hire a live musician to create a buddy action soundtrack that you can use for your shows. I have found it is ultimately more cost effective to have someone improvising our sound and lights from the booth rather than having to hire a musician for every show.
- It's helpful to create a library of genre-appropriate sound effects to have at your fingertips. (A note about guns and gunshots: in general, the buddies shouldn't be shooting anyone. There are many ways to introduce action in a story like this—slow-motion fighting, chases, and so on. Shooting someone point-blank is not something anyone wants to see on an improv stage—or anywhere.)

Lights

In advance of the show, set playing areas that the actors will go to for different types of locations. For example, instead of the actors quickly moving chairs around in the partial darkness, have two chairs placed downstage left or right that can easily be a car, or a bed, or seats in the chief's office. Create specific lighting for these areas in advance. You will want to have a full wash of light on the stage at some points, but at other points you may want to focus on a certain area that is more intimate or helps create the feeling that we are changing locations. Tech your set just as you would a play. Have the actors rehearse in the areas and know what is available to them.

The key to this genre is relationship first, action second. Don't get caught up in the details of the crime. The plots of action films are barely remembered. It's the characters we care about.

13

FISH-OUT-OF-WATER IMPROVISED FILMS AND TELEVISION SHOWS

Stories have long thrived on a plot device in which our hero or heroes find themselves entirely out of their depth in a new environment. This versatile device allows extraordinary things to happen to ordinary people. If you are like a fish out of water, you feel awkward because you are in an unfamiliar situation or because the people you are with are very different from you. Chaucer used a version of this phrase in *The Canterbury Tales*: "A monk, when he is cloisterless; is like to a fish that is waterless."

In this style of story, the hero is an outsider, and we follow their POV. They make the world they enter better than how they found it—which is different from the outsider in a typical noir story because in this case they usually bring destruction and chaos. Fish-out-of-water stories usually end happily for all involved.

Here are some *great* TV and film examples of an outsider coming in to an established environment.

- *Ted Lasso*
- *Schitt's Creek* (The entire Rose family is made up of fishes out of water.)
- *Doc Martin*
- *Ugly Betty*
- *The Englishman Who Went Up a Hill and Came Down a Mountain*
- *Hot Fuzz*

A common trope in these stories has a big-city person or persons sent on a mission to a small town. Even though we follow our lead throughout, it is essential to note that the inhabitants and the small town or village itself are the heart of the story. We must care about them and their future. For an improvised story, I find it helpful to introduce the village first and then add the outsider, but you can practice both ways. You can have an opening scene where the outsider receives their mission and then heads to the village. In *Schitt's Creek*, we meet the Rose family first before they are thrust into the town of Schitt's Creek, and then we gradually meet its inhabitants. In *Ted Lasso*, the village is a football club the outsider has come to lead.

Most of the notes and suggestions in this chapter are based on the fish-out-of-water film *An Englishman Who Went Up a Hill and Came Down a Mountain*, a single, self-contained story rather than a TV series with multiple episodes. Once you've done an improvised film, consider trying a multiweek run of an improvised series. Just like a soap opera, in a series the performers get to know their characters very well, and that is a huge plus.

The Village

When you improvise your story, you'll want to begin by asking your audience what the village is known for—for example, a special bread recipe, a waterfall, a yearly festival?

In this genre, the villagers will all be quirky characters with strong wants and eccentricities. What unites all of these oddballs is their love for the village. Depending on how the story develops, the villagers may be admirable either for their desire to preserve the town the way it has always been or for their willingness to embrace progress.

In the small village or town in this kind of story, what you do defines your character. Depending on the country you choose and the era you pick, these jobs may or may not exist nowadays, but will give you a sense of what is possible.

- pub or bar owner
- watchmaker, clockmaker
- blacksmith, mason, bricklayer
- baker, bread maker
- minister, preacher
- shipwright, carpenter
- chemist, pharmacist, doctor
- lamplighter
- tailor, seamstress, hatter, cobbler
- weaver
- telegraph operator, postal worker
- barber, hair stylist
- train station operator
- coffin maker

The Outsider

The outsider is sent to this small village from a large city like London or New York. Possible reasons why they are coming to *this* village may include the following:

- They've inherited a house, building, farm, or church in the village or the village itself.
- They're trying to hide (for a specified, brief amount of time).
- They were invited by one or more residents or local leaders.
- They're offering a product that competes with something that the village makes or is comparably high-tech (like a tractor or a loom (depending on the era) that could bring problems as well as benefits.
- They want to take something from the village that the village is known for.
- They want to build a road, rail line, canal, or something else that will divide the village in two.
- They are a surveyor who has come to verify or adjust a boundary, which could change which county the town is in, divide the village in two, or cause some other disruption.
- They are a historian, novelist, poet, or journalist looking for story ideas or for information related to a particular story.
- They're scouting the village as a location for a movie.
- They want to compete in an annual town contest that has never involved an outsider (e.g., a horse race, another sporting event, or something agricultural).
- They are a new priest or minister or vicar appointed to a local church temporarily.

- They are bringing the body of a former resident who died in the city and wanted to be buried in the village—perhaps someone whom the locals disliked or had forgotten.

Whatever the outsider's reasons for being there, their purpose will shape the arc of the story. If, for example, the village is known for its soap and an outsider wants the recipe for the soap, the villagers might provide the recipe and then regret it; or go to great lengths to keep the recipe from the outsider; or debate what to do as this has never happened before; or do something else entirely. The outsider needs only to keep trying to get what they want and to change their tactics when they are thwarted.

Often thrown into all of this is a rom-com aspect. The outsider is almost always involved in a romantic entanglement that changes them and the village somehow. Perhaps it will be because of the love they have for this villager that they will either help the village (as in *The Englishman Who Went Up a Hill and Came Down a Mountain*), or the town will be changed in some positive way.

Three-Act Structure

You can stick to this structure in your rehearsal process, but as the ensemble gets more comfortable with the conventions of the genre, loosen up the scene order and story structure for more organic story-telling. These are training wheels only.

Act 1

- Scene 1: A narrator walks out into a pool of light. They name the village and what it is known for based on the prompt from the audience. This is short and underscored with music from your tech. (Having a narrator is not necessary, but it's great for emulating the feeling of a film like *The Englishman Who Went Up a Hill and Came Down a Mountain*. Either everyone in the ensemble becomes adept at this, or one person is designated to narrate at the beginning and close of every show.)

- Scene 2: Develop key townsfolk and their relationships, situations, and dreams.
- Scene 3: The outsider arrives. Their objective is based on what the improviser has seen so far. What will cause the most disruption in this village? It can be giving the locals what they want or not.
- Scene 4: We see interactions between the outsider and townsfolk and perhaps some scenes with townsfolk only. The outsider's objective is either known to the villagers or kept secret. However, keeping it vague for the other improvisers can be lethal so do make it clear to them and the audience. Whether the villagers know the truth or not can be played different ways depending on the story.
- End of act 1: Some sort of turning point, which will be different in each story. Maybe the outsider's arrival itself is a huge turning point. Perhaps the revelation of the outsider's plan is the turning point. Perhaps the outsider's realization that this isn't going to be as fast or easy as they expected is the turning point. This works best if it also involves a realization or decision by the townsfolk.

Act 2

- Scenes may happen concurrently or in quick succession at an accelerating pace.

- The outsider continues pursuing their objective while the villagers' relationships with each other and the outsider keep developing.

- At the end of act 2 there should be some sort of turning point in the relationship between the outsider and the townsfolk (or at least one important townsperson—usually a town leader, a local adversary, or a romantic interest). This could be the outsider receiving help from an unexpected source, the start of a romance (usually a first kiss), the first clear moment of sympathy the outsider feels toward the town or vice versa, and so on. Note: If things have been going badly for the outsider, this turning point should probably be a turn for the better; if things have been going well, it is probably a turn for the worse.

Act 3

- There are further scenes happening at an increasing pace with developments between specific characters affecting other characters and the course of the story.

- There is a further development of all relationships and a deepening pursuit of the outsider's objective.

- All of this builds toward a climax, after which the outsider, the village, or both, find themselves changed for the better. If the outsider has had a romantic relationship, it is resolved happily.

- The narrator from the beginning may return to close the show and reflect on "how things are and will be from now on."

Notes on Music

- Before the show, immerse your waiting audience in energized music that will get everyone in the mood for a delightful, comic romp. When we did this genre in the era of *The Englishman Who Went Up a Hill and Came Down a Mountain*, we had fiddle music playing before and throughout the show to really give a sense of time and place.
- Music is also vital for scene transitions: bring the volume up and down to smooth things out and create continuity.
- Montages must have music to underscore the action. If you have a scene that takes place at a music festival or a pub with live music, be sure to build your music library based on the time period and location of your village.

Specific Scene Types

Group Scenes

Group scenes are great energizers and can help to clarify elements of the story. They also help to give a sense of life in the village as a whole. Practice these extensively because they require a second circle group mindset to not become a mess. Things to keep in mind:

- Possible environments can include a pub, a town hall, a local music festival, a wedding, a funeral, a church bazaar, or a holiday such as May Day, Guy Fawkes Day, and so forth.

- If the scene is in a pub, it can be a great opportunity for the group to sing or dance together. Memorize the melody to "Knees Up Mother Brown" and practice improvising to it. Era-appropriate folk dances might include the Circle, Pinwheel, London Bridges, and Partners. There are many other great examples on the Internet.

- The outsider's objective and motivation must be explicit by the time the group scene begins. That *want*, and the villager's reactions to it, fuel the scene.

- Be careful what you "Yes, and" in this scene. I've seen group scenes start strong only to have everyone jumping in by providing side comments that end up changing the outsider's want. Keep the outsider's goal simple and don't try to make it more elaborate in this scene. If the group is arguing about how to deal with the outsider, the crux of that argument can't keep changing directions. Keep going deeper into what is already established; have your own reaction to it, but don't try to change what the outsider wants. Likewise, if the group plans to try to fool the outsider somehow, don't get too complicated. It shouldn't be preposterous. It may be enough just to distract the outsider with one person while the rest are doing something to thwart them.

Montage

Montages can be an effective way to move the story ahead, whether depicting people building something, working to hide a supply of something from the outsider, or doing anything else physical with the music played loud and no one talking. It consists of very short scenes (lights quickly up and down), ending in the climax. A good example is the building of the mountain in *The Englishman Who Went Up a Hill and Came Down a Mountain.*

Whatever era you choose for your improvised fish-out-of-water film or series, the best aspects of the genre are the potential transformations of all involved. In *Ugly Betty*, Betty not only changes everyone around her for the better, she becomes more fully herself (the village in this case is *Mode Magazine*). The inclusive nature of *Schitt's Creek* and *Ugly Betty* will allow rich narratives to develop with your ensemble.

The joy and connection at the end of these improv stories stays with me long after the show is over. The audience and the improvisers leave the theater smiling. Improv theater has the potential to connect us at the deepest level.

In Closing

Narrative improv has challenged me to my core and required me to look at myself as honestly as I can. It reminds me, time and again, that the sole (soul) purpose of our lives is to connect to ourselves, others, and to something greater than all of us.

It reminds me of a visceral feeling I have when I meditate, of three phases of connection. When I'm first sitting, I'm in My Story. There is a dome over me that is very close to my body. I'm wrapped up in the details of my life, but as I sit longer, I begin to open. My energy field expands, and that next layer is Our Story. This is when I'm either connecting to others in the room or sending love to loved ones or even those I'm in conflict with. As I sit longer, I open even more, and the biggest dome is The Story. I am connected to myself, others around me or in my mind, and then finally to all beings and The Story.

This is also the place where improv magic happens: connected to yourself, to those you are improvising with—including your tech team and audience—and open to something bigger than yourself.

My Story

Our Story

The Story

Don't hesitate to reach out. I'm here.

Jo McGinley

improjo@gmail.com

www.westcoastschoolofimprov.com

Index